A TRAVEL HANDBOOK
FOR MUSLIMS

# Souvenir *of* *Taqwā*

ABEER ARAIN

Souvenir of *Taqwā: A travel Handbook for Muslims*

*First Published in 2025 by*
Kube Publishing Ltd

*Distributed by*
KUBE PUBLISHING LTD
MCC, Ratby Lane,
Markfield, Leicestershire. LE67 9SY
Tel +44 (0)1530 249230
E-mail: info@kubepublishing.com
Website: www.kubepublishing.com



*Editor:* Salman Al-Azami

*Cover Design and Typesetting:* Afreen Fazil (Jaryah Studios)

A Cataloguing-in-Publication Data record for this book is available from the British Library

ISBN: 978-1-84774-260-5 Paperback
ISBN 978-1-84774-261-2 Ebook

Printed by: Elma Basim, Turkey

# Contents

# Introduction

*"Do not be like those who forgot Allah, so He made them forget their own selves."* (Qur'an 59:19)

Our transient time in this *dunya* (lower world) is like being at the airport. Imagine arriving at one of the best airports on the planet. There are luxuries and comforts all around, from delicious cuisines to elegant ambiance – it is a gratifying place to be in. We enjoy the spectacular panoramic views and delight in the delicious menus. However, none of us would claim the airport to be our final destination. It is only a temporary station where we are vigilant about our departure times. The announcement to board the flight may come at any moment. Such is our life in this *dunya*. Here, we earn money, spend time with family and friends, strive for success and travel. There is ease and prosperity within reach. Money can buy us a comfortable life. However, death is inevitable. The sole purpose of this *dunya* is to take us to our final destination. We all have a predetermined time to leave, to head towards the next phase. As Allah says in the Qur'an, "*O my people, this life of the world is only a (momentary) benefit, while the Hereafter is, indeed, the place of permanent living*" (Qur'an 40:39).

Even though our time on this earth is temporary, we are enjoined to seek knowledge, get married, raise a family and strive for a comfortable lifestyle. To help us live according to what pleases Him, Allah ﷻ has given us the Qur'an as a guidebook and the Prophet ﷺ as a role model. They both show us how to live a balanced life while staying mindful of our ultimate destination, *Ākhirah* (the Hereafter).

As humans, we naturally have a desire to see and experience the world. We have a built-in inclination to travel and explore the beauty of our planet. Travelling in and of itself is not futile – it broadens our horizons. Visiting far-off places, encountering new customs and cultures, liberates us from our biases and limitations. Long voyages can open the gates of knowledge through observations and inquisitiveness. However, if we are not careful, leisure travel can distract us from what is paramount, *taqwā* (consciousness of Allah's presence) even while enjoying worldly pleasures.

How can we maintain our focus on *Ākhirah* during our travels, when material attractions surround us from all directions? The answer lies in redirecting the compass of our hearts towards Allah. *Taqwā* revitalizes our connection with Allah and nourishes the soul. The soul can only find peace and contentment when it is conscious of the presence of its Creator.

This handbook, *Souvenir of Taqwā*, aims to make our travel experiences worthwhile by helping us stay connected with Allah ﷻ and follow His commands. It encourages us to rethink our travel habits and explore ways to refresh our *iman* (faith) through travel. Every good deed we perform in our lives can become an act of worship, simply by changing our intentions. With this book, Muslim travellers will be inspired to discover new landscapes with greater consciousness and appreciate the beauty of *taqwā* as they behold the beautiful world created by Allah ﷻ. This handbook synthesizes traditional Islamic knowledge with practical advice to help travellers prioritize *taqwā* during their leisure journeys. Readers will be better equipped to create a thoughtful itinerary that addresses the why, how and when of their travels.

*"Have they not traveled in the land where they could have seen how was the fate of those before them? And surely the abode of the Hereafter is much better for those who fear Allah. Would you, then, still not understand?" (Qur'an 12:109)*

# Travel in Islam: A Brief History

Travel was an integral component in developing the Islamic sciences and Islamic civilization itself. As Muslims travelled, they recorded descriptions of the lands and peoples they encountered. Fascinating details about climate, customs, religions and the daily rituals of the world's people facilitated the production of knowledge and theory across nations.

## The Spread of Islam Through Travel

*"And He is the One Who has made the stars as your guide through the darkness of land and sea. We have already made the signs clear for people who know."* (Qur'an 6:97)

Many historians and social scientists consider Islam to be the first true global civilization and attribute this partly to the widespread travels of Muslim scholars.[1] Muslim travel paved the way for the spread of knowledge, technological advancements and the exchange of culture along the way. Travel has been a part of the spread of Islam since Islam's inception. The prime intention for travel was to invite others to the message of Islam. When the Prophet ﷺ was in Makkah, he sent Mus'ab ibn Umayr to Madinah for *dawah* (invitation) to Islam. Mus'ab lived in Madinah and successfully spread the message of the Prophet ﷺ to a wide majority. As a result, when the Prophet ﷺ migrated to Madinah, a large population of Muslims was there to welcome him to his new home. He also sent other companions to far-away lands, including Muadh ibn Jabal to Yemen. The Prophet ﷺ instructed him to be tolerant in his speech and not to use harsh words or alienate the local population of the area (Bukhari 2873). Muadh visited various places in Yemen, maximizing his dawah efforts through travel. Soon the region of Hadramawt became a hub for travelling scholars and merchants. Mosques were built and Islam thrived in the region, from where it spread to the East, into Asia. The Prophet ﷺ also sent letters to different statesmen through his companions, who travelled to faraway lands and observed unfamiliar cultures.

Muslims have historically migrated for various reasons, such as seeking refuge, conquering new lands or undertaking scholarship. In the era of the first four caliphs, Islamic power and authority was consolidated and Muslims began living in the far-off lands of Syria, Persia, Egypt and North Africa. Many companions of the Prophet ﷺ were assigned governorship duties in these lands. As Muslims prospered in the newly occupied lands, a new generation of scholars arose from or travelled to these lands to learn jurisprudence and hadith from the companions of the Prophet ﷺ.

Muslim migration, however, started long before the conquests on the battlefield and played a crucial role in the spread of Islam in its early years.[2] The first migration made by Muslims was to Abyssinia, followed by other voluntary migrations in the early Islamic period, before the second major migration (*hijra*) to Madinah. After the time of the Prophet ﷺ, Muslims continued to migrate for different purposes – scholarly pursuits were most common. Renowned scholars, such as Imam Bukhari, spent most of their lives travelling to collect *hadiths* (reports about the life of the Prophet and his companions). Al-Ghazali, another prominent scholar and ascetic, also travelled multiple times during his lifetime.

Trade played a significant role in the expansion of Islam beyond the lands of the Arabs. The Prophet ﷺ and his companions travelled for trade, as it was a major part of business in the Arabian Peninsula. Muslim traders, through their commercial exchanges, extended the spread of Islam across the Indian Ocean, the Silk Route and Western seaports. During their travels, Muslim merchants introduced others to their beliefs, values and Islamic way of life, which further extended Islam in those regions. In addition to trade, Muslims also travelled for spiritual practices, particularly towards central Asia, for training in Sufism (spiritual purification).[3] These areas still have the remains of Islamic monuments dating back to the fifteenth century.

Muslims have historically travelled as merchants, explorers and voyagers. It was vital for them to know the details of flora and fauna, along with the geography of the area, as people moved from place to place with their herd or came to Makkah for pilgrimage. Al-Khwarizmi, a ninth-century scholar from what is now Uzbekistan, was one of the earliest geographers from the Muslim world. His book, *The Form of the Earth*, inspired a generation of writers and explorers.[4]

During the medieval Islamic period, Muslims excelled in the field of science. Muslim scientists took special interest in navigation and explained astronomical principles to make travelling easier. One notable contribution was from Marium al-Asturlabiyy, a tenth-century astronomer who worked with her father to invent the astrolabe.[5] After her father's death she continued to work on the project and developed sophisticated astrolabes during an apprenticeship in Aleppo, Syria. The astrolabe helped with timekeeping and celestial calculations and also assisted with prayer times and establishing the direction of Makkah. Compact astrolabes were used for navigational purposes, solving many problems for travellers and explorers during that time.

*"Do they then not travel through the Earth, so that their minds gain wisdom and their ears thus learn to hear?* (Qur'an 2:46)

## Prominent Muslim Travellers from the Medieval Period

The medieval Islamic period had many prominent travellers who not only travelled extensively but also wrote about their journeys and later compiled them into manuscripts. The eighth-century traveller Al-Yaqubi wrote *The Book of Countries*.[6] In his travelogue, he documented the names of the places he visited, the distances between them and their topography. He also took note of the tax system and water resources. His accounts of China and its aquatic wildlife were exceptionally detailed. Another famous name from the eighth century was Al-Muqaddisi, a geographer and traveller who set out on a journey from his hometown, Jerusalem and recorded notes as he travelled across the Muslim world. Al-Muqaddisi wrote an excellent travelogue called *Best Divisions for Knowledge of Regions*, which he completed later in the eighth century.[7] Some parts of this book are still available in various languages. Like other travellers in his time, divine inspiration played a vital role in his journeys and he travelled to see the world created by Allah Almighty.

During the tenth century, part of the Islamic golden age, Muslim travellers embarked on journeys to far-off places and elevated the standards of travel literature. They provided notes to accompany their maps and included lengthy commentaries about all they witnessed in the new towns. Abu al-Qasim ibn Hawqal wrote one such commentary in his book *Kitab Surat al-Ardh* (The Book of the Shape of the Earth).[8] He carefully described the golden age of al-Andalus (Muslim Spain), including its modern irrigation systems, trading centers and excellent quality of life. He also examined their books of banking and accounting and observed the system of promissory notes called *shakk* (modern-day "cheque"). Such institutions were unheard of in other parts of the world at that time.[8]

In the same century Muslims were travelling to the far North. The most probable first was the Arab chronicler Ibn Fadlan. As an Arab envoy and a diplomat, he was sent north from Baghdad by the Abbasid caliph Al-Muqtadir. The purpose of his journey was to meet with the Muslim community in the north and teach them the basic principles and practices of Islam. Ibn Fadlan wrote an account of his travels in his book *Risalah*, a gripping narrative that still stands out in Arabic literature for its flavour and balanced description of the lives of the people he met. He encountered Viking traders upon reaching the Volga River and noted meticulous descriptions of their customs, cultural practices and religion.[9] Ibn Fadlan also noted his experience of the northern lights and mentioned the difficulty of fitting the prayer times during short winter days. Another Muslim traveller from the tenth century was Ibn Khurradadhbih, who wrote *The Book of Roads and Provinces*, describing his travels to the Far East towards modern-day Japan, Korea and Indonesia.[10]

In the twelfth century, *The Gift of the Hearts and the Bouquet of Wonders* became immensely popular.[11] It was a travel account of Abu Hamid al-Andalusi, who spent twenty-four years exploring Sasqin, Bulghar and modern-day Hungary. His book was a collection of descriptions of the natural and man-made wonders he encountered during his travels. He too, like Ibn Fadlan, utilized his opportunity to spread Islam. Another prominent writer in the twelfth century was Al-Bakri, a minister in Seville, Spain. He was an essayist and wrote a detailed geographical outline of the Arabian peninsula, along with the names of towns, valleys and monuments, in his book *Routes and Kingdoms*.[12] As time elapsed, common people also began documenting their Hajj journeys and recording their encounters with diverse cultures, the outcome of which was an expansive collection of travel writings and manuscripts.[13] Scholars dedicated themselves to the study of geography. They were inspired by the curiosity of their surroundings and their knowledge of faith.

In the twelfth century, the scholar Al-Idrisi produced a detailed atlas of the known continents, including Asia, Europe and North Africa. This was a one-of-a-kind map during that time, centuries before Marco Polo set out on his journey.[14] Al-Idrisi drew on his geographical knowledge and that of travellers to the region to get the correct details on his atlas. He also calculated the Earth's circumference as 22,900 miles at the equator, only about ten percent off from the measurements since established.

From the thirteenth century we have the example of Yaqut al-Hamawi, a geographer who wrote the *Dictionary of Countries* about the towns and cities he visited and outlined their monuments, resources, history and populations.[15] Ibn Saeed al-Maghribi was another traveller who expertly gave an account of the latitude and longitude of each place he visited in the Indian Ocean islands. Ibn al-Faqih also travelled to India and China and compared their foods, rituals, clothing and customs.[16]

It was in the fourteenth century that the most famous Muslim traveller, Ibn Battuta, set out on his journey. He left Tangier, Morocco, at the age of twenty-two to perform Hajj. However, fate had a different plan for him. Ibn Battuta travelled for twenty-nine long years before returning to his hometown. His travelogues and the details of his journeys make him one of the most famous travellers in history. Through his writing, one can envision so much of the medieval world, from Egypt and Syria to the far east of China. During his journey, Ibn Battuta worked as a jurist, trader and scholar and stayed as a guest of sultans and emperors. At the request of the Sultan of Fez, he completed his book *Rihla.*[17] Many historians have written biographies of Ibn Battuta and translators have made what survives of his travel writing available in different languages.

In the early nineteenth century, another Muslim travelogue became popular: the book of the Egyptian cleric Rifa'a Rafi al-Tahtawi on his journey to Paris, where he recorded his impressions of French culture.[18] There, Imam al-Tahtawi saw museums for the first time, describing them as storehouses that help scholars preserve their knowledge of history, natural sciences, botany and wildlife.

Muslim scholars and scientists continued to travel throughout the medieval Islamic period and enriched the literary world.[19] New ideas and scientific advances in other fields of knowledge, such as minerals and rocks, also reached the Islamic world through travelling scholars. Muslim voyagers satiated their desire for learning through travel, thus becoming a powerful force in the creation of an interconnected Islamic civilization.[20]

> ***Say, "Travel in the land and look how He has originated the creation. Then Allah will create the subsequent creation. Surely Allah is powerful to do everything." (Qur'an 29:19)***

# Basic Principles of Travel

"Leave your country in search of loftiness and travel! For in travel there are five benefits: relief of adversity, earning of livelihood, knowledge, etiquette and noble companionship." (Imam Shafi'i)

## Travel is Not a Waste of Time

*"Say, O Prophet, "Travel throughout the land and see how He originated the creation, then Allah will bring it into being one more time. Surely, Allah is Most Capable of everything."* (Qur'an 29:20)

For a Muslim, travelling is in three categories. The first is for religious purposes, which involves visiting Makkah, Madinah and Jerusalem (al-Aqsa Mosque). The second category is for gaining knowledge, such as visiting historical places that the Prophet ﷺ had visited or other sites from the Islamic golden era. The third category is travelling for leisure, which involves exploring scenic landscapes and countryside destinations. All forms of travel can be beneficial to Muslims. However, it is not uncommon to hear people say that any travel except for religious purposes is a waste of time. While religious pilgrimages are undoubtedly the superior form of travel, through which one earns rewards even when en-route, recreational travel, too, is not useless. Like everything else, our leisure time also depends on how we use it.

In the modern era, the world has shrunk into a small global village. Travel is not what it used to be, requiring a jump into the unknown and unimaginable. Hence, the excitement is not the same. We now can learn about our destinations in printed guidebooks and on social media. However, the idea of travel continues to enthrall human minds. In the high-tech world of live streams and vlogs, travel still widens our lens and makes us see the world in a larger context. It provides a quick break from the monotony of our daily routine and nurtures the seeds of imagination and excitement. It is a form of education like no other, with memories that stay with us for a lifetime. Sometimes, life's greatest lessons are learned during travel through unforgettable experiences. The one thing to remember about travel is that it is never a waste of time. While there may be challenges during travel, conquering them is an invaluable experience for our personal development. Complications during travel help us understand our capabilities and shortcomings. Some people discover new passions and interests from their travel, while others gain a better understanding of themselves. Travelling offers moments of joy, insight and a better perception of life, all of which are beneficial in developing our personality and character.

*"Travelling leaves you speechless, then turns you into a storyteller."* Ibn Battuta

Our routine typically keeps us in a self-created comfort zone. It is our place of safety and satisfaction, a haven for abstraction and reality. Most of us, as a result, tend to put off travelling and exploring until retirement, when we have more time on our hands. However, there is a need to rebuild our mental strength even when life's business keeps us occupied. It is often necessary to get out from under the comfort blanket and get to know the unknown. That's where travel comes in. It awakens our inner curiosity and opens the doors of experience and knowledge. Ultimately, the appreciation we get from travelling reenergizes us to return to our scheduled activities with zeal and enthusiasm.

*"It is only in adventure that some people succeed in knowing themselves – in finding themselves."* Andre Gide

To travel is to get to know oneself. One learns more about their traits when on a journey than during their normal life. Travelling may expose us to anxiety, impulse-buying or insights into how we make decisions. It provides one of the best lessons on self-assessment, provided that we carefully observe our behaviour, before pointing fingers at others. On the spiritual side, we may also become aware of our reliance on Allah, how much we remember Him and how grateful we are for His blessings upon us. Interestingly, we also learn about others by travelling with them. Once, during the time of Caliph Umar ibn al-Khattab, a witness was brought for inquiry during the prosecution of a criminal case. Umar asked the witness, "Were you with him (the accused) on a journey as a result of which you come to know his character?" The man said, "I was not." Umar said, "Then I think you do not know him."[1] The Caliph said this because long journeys reveal character flaws in conflicts and unusual events. In the absence of life's comforts and family members, true personalities can show. As someone wisely said, "if you want to know someone, travel with them". Travelling can help us clarify which friendships in life are truly meaningful for our *Ākhirah*. It allows us to focus on those relationships which remind us of Allah.

## Know Your "Why"

*"Yet all this is no more than a 'fleeting' enjoyment in this worldly life. But the Hereafter with your Lord is only for those mindful of Him."* (Qur'an 43:35)

The first step in travelling is to make a decision to go and the second step is to determine the reason for the trip. Why do we want to go on a trip? Does the destination play any role in our decision to travel or does it not matter where we go? Will it be for relaxation, self-reflection, adventure or learning a new skill? Should we visit our family home or explore an unfamiliar culture?

Every journey starts with the unknown; however, questioning oneself before beginning to plan ensures successful outcomes from the trip. The Japanese concept of *ikigai*, which means to pursue your passion, emphasizes the significance of asking some primary questions which can also be applied to travel: what you are good at, what the world needs from you and what you love. Asking these questions opens our minds to experience new places, cultures and things.

At times, the first assumptions about a trip may prove to be wrong. Two questions, however, help us here. First, is our trip for travel or a vacation? Second, are we going to be tourists or travellers on this trip? Any journey away from work, stressful routine at home or mundane tasks can be a vacation. Tourists seek respite from their busy lives and expect relaxation. On the contrary, a trip for adventure, exploration or learning is travel. Some travellers prioritize gaining experience or education and can handle a relatively tiresome trip. Thus, categorizing the trip can help avoid disappointments. Whether we are looking forward to having a mini-luxe stay at a resort or wanting to know about geological details of the forest, is up to us. Additionally, when multiple people plan a trip together, such as a group of cousins or an entire family, it becomes necessary to consider everyone's anticipations and goals for the trip. This will help in planning the itinerary, as discussed later in this book. An ideal trip is not about having a perfect roadmap; rather, it aims to inculcate personal connections, find harmony in personal and work life and achieve specific travel goals, all without neglecting our prime duties as a Muslim.

For Muslims, the "why" of travel is incomplete without *ikhlas (sincerity)*, that is to direct our *niyah* (intention) towards pleasing Allah ﷻ and obtaining rewards. Whether it is travelling or spending time with family, the direction of our *niyah* must be towards Allah ﷻ. This is because the opposite of *ikhlas* would come under *riya* (ostentation), which is considered a minor *shirk* (associating partners with Allah). The Prophet ﷺ, said, "What I fear for you (his *ummah*) is the minor *shirk*, that is *ar-riya*. On the Day of Judgment, Allah ﷻ will say when rewarding the people for their actions, "Go to those for whom you did *riya* in the world, then see if you find the reward with them."[2]

Travelling and learning new things while exploring Allah's ﷻ wide earth is beautiful. It can be a rewarding experience if the intentions are pure. As Muslims, every journey that evokes our spiritual focus becomes a way to please Allah ﷻ. Travelling can be as quick as visiting relatives or friends in neighbouring areas to maintain ties of kinship or going far away to provide help to those in need during natural disasters. One may also visit the sick, earning the focus of angels who supplicate for those who meet their fellows to console them when they are ill or aggrieved. One may also travel to earn a halal livelihood to spend on family or charity. As Muslims, we also earn rewards if we travel to obtain knowledge and intend to help humanity with our research. We may also travel to meet with the scholars who have dedicated their lives to the path of Allah ﷻ. Travel can be with one's spouse and children, to take care of their needs as it pleases Allah ﷻ or for oneself, to attain good health by going out in nature and observing the Almighty's Magnificence. There are benefits to be derived from observing new lands and beautiful gardens, hearing new languages and seeing new ethnicities. Finally, the most superior form of travel, where one earns rewards even during the journey, is for religious purposes. It involves going on the pilgrimage and visiting the holy sites of Masjid al-Haram, Masjid al-Nabawi and Masjid al-Aqsa.

In his book, *The Revival of the Religious Sciences,* Al-Ghazali strictly classified travelling into two categories: optional versus obligatory. Travelling for the worldly purpose of gaining fame, name and wealth is optional, whereas religious travel to visit Makkah, Madinah or Jerusalem is virtuous and a source of rewards. Al-Ghazali further categorized the recommended form of travel into travel for knowledge, for rectifying one's character and for seeing Allah's ﷻ wonderful creations.

*"No soul can ever die without Allah's Will at a destined time. Those who desire worldly gain, We will let them have it and those who desire heavenly reward, We will grant it to them. And We will reward those who are grateful."* (Qur'an 3:145)

The Prophet ﷺ said, "Actions are but by the intention and every man will have but that which he intended. So he whose emigration was for Allah and His Messenger, his emigration was for Allah and His Messenger. But he whose emigration was for some worldly benefit or to take some woman in marriage, his emigration was for that which he emigrated." (Ibn Majah 4227)

Our travels in this world are examples of our final return to the Almighty. Therefore, the objective of our worldly trips must be to direct our attention towards the Hereafter. A Muslim traveller learns from the signs of Allah during travel and avoids the distractions that may tilt our focus from *ikhlas*.

"Two roads diverged in a wood and I,

I took the one less travelled by." – Robert Frost

## A Well-crafted Itinerary

*"Whatever good you do, Allah will know it. Take provisions along, for the merit of (having) provision is to abstain (from begging) and fear Me, O men of understanding!"* (Qur'an 2:197)

The literal meaning of itinerary is the planned schedule of events for an upcoming trip – a time-consuming but crucial step. Every traveller adopts a different style when it comes to mapping out the designated areas to see during the trip. Some may take hours and days to figure out a few basics about their destination, while others quickly look up the basics and prefer to go with the flow. Even though we learn most about a place only after exploring it, a pre-planned itinerary is still a prerequisite to avoid over-exhaustion and boredom. No doubt, easy access to information in current times has made this step very doable, yet we would still benefit from a few lists before setting out on a journey. In a broad sense, the plan usually is to visit a place that is reachable, safe and within one's budget. Timing, weather conditions and political situations at the desired location are also to be considered.

## Weather

This is often a good start when an itinerary is planned. Look up what weather you can expect. When are the harsh winter months or the hottest summer heat? The chosen destination must be feasible during one's travel window. One may also want to be aware of any health risks associated with the area, for example, high asbestos exposure, poor quality air or any other outbreak common in the area.

## Booking

Any trip other than a road trip in one's own vehicle requires the booking of a flight, train or bus ride. Pre-booking saves time and money and, contrary to popular belief, flights can often be cheaper when purchased only a few weeks ahead of time. One can also compare prices between airports – sometimes, it may be cheaper to fly to a bigger city and rent a car or take a train to the destination. Be sure to avoid planning too tightly, so you can have some extra time to visit local markets or try street food. One should also try to begin their journey on a Thursday to follow the *sunnah* of our Prophet ﷺ who preferred setting out on Thursdays (Bukhari 2950).

## Mode of Transportation

What are the standard modes of transportation at our destination? Is one headed to an island that does not have rental cars or is it a must to rent a vehicle? Similarly, there are areas where walking may be the best way to explore, such as in smaller towns or hill stations.

## Accommodation

Options for accommodation may vary, depending on the traveller's lifestyle, budget and personal preferences. Some prefer staying at a resort, while those who travel with family may rent an entire apartment. Solo travellers might prefer a rental share with family, friends and relatives instead of expensive lodging. When choosing a hotel or rental home, there are a few basic points to look for, such as the distance from the airport, the safety of the area and the hotel's legitimacy – online reviews and photos shared by other travellers are helpful in this case. Unless you're travelling in peak season, it might not be necessary to have a hotel booking for the whole time and then you can have the flexibility of choosing a new hotel as you explore. However, some countries require that you prove you have a booking for the entire stay.

## Demographics

Knowing the general demographics of the visiting place is helpful, especially for Muslims. One may want to note if there is any Muslim community or an Islamic center at the destination. Similarly, language barriers and the need for an interpreter should also be considered before travelling, for our safety.

## Restaurants

Next, list places for breakfast and lunch and their hours of operation. Finding halal options and looking for a *zabiha* (slaughtered Islamically) halal certificate on the website makes finding our meals easier. While online reviews may be helpful, one must not be too stern when it comes to food reviews, as reviews are often influenced by personal eating habits and cuisine preferences. One may still give a chance to a restaurant and try its food.

## Points of Interest

Every place has something special to offer, whether we are in Buraydah, Saudi Arabia, known for its world-class palm date festival or Cappadocia in Türkiye, famous for its hot air balloon festival. In today's world, every town or city offers at least one unique experience to its visitors. Some places are known for open museums, like the mining museum in Butte, Colorado, USA, while others have special history museums for children, like in Manchester, UK. Some places have long waiting lists for reservations, such as hotels inside national parks. Once you know what interests you, you can make a list of must-visit places, including mosques, nature areas, botanical gardens, safari parks, bookstores, libraries and more. Jotting down opening hours, ticket prices and the distance between the hotel or rental home and the selected area can also save time during the trip.

## Festivals and Events

It's important to check for major events and festivals that may take place during the intended period of stay. These could include sports events, art fairs, food festivals, book fairs or other cultural events. Looking for an Islamic conference during travel dates would also be a good idea, as one may join a gathering where Allah is remembered. Peak seasons, however, come with a few disadvantages, such as expensive accommodation and limited availability due to high demand. Therefore, having an idea of the timing of peak seasons at our destination is helpful so we may plan the itinerary accordingly.

## Packing

As some of the experienced travellers say, our packing choices can make or break our trip. For solo travellers, packing may not be too difficult, but during family trips, over-packing and heavier luggage can become a dilemma. The luggage we carry depends on the destination's weather, the size and weight requirements of the airline and our personal preferences. While large duffel bags may be tempting, they often get too heavy and do not provide enough back support. Instead, sturdy suitcases and weather-proof backpacks are good choices, especially for children. To make packing easier, it is always helpful to create a packing list where one can write items down and tick them off as they pack. Packing lists are also provided by online applications like PackPoint, Packr and Packing Pro, to name a few.

## Travel Documents

No travel is done without travel documents, i.e., passport, identification card and driver's license. The list also includes tickets (printed or saved online), discount passes and health and travel insurance cards. However, one document that is often overlooked is an advance directive card. It can be an official document or a self-written card containing information about the traveller's advance directives in case of an accident or sudden death. This is particularly crucial for Muslims, especially when travelling to non-Muslim countries. The advance directive card can include religious preferences and contact information for the nearest Islamic center.

***"...and no one knows in which land he will die." (Qur'an 31:34)***

While pre-planning and taking notes are helpful, there is no such thing as a perfect travel itinerary. There is always a possibility that things may change during the trip, such as inclement weather at national parks or an unexpected renovation at the museum that may alter our day's entire travel plan. One may also find your planned stops less interesting than what you spontaneously find along the way. Sometimes it won't be worth staying in one town or city for a whole week and we may want to explore neighbouring areas.

Expert travellers suggest balancing between pre-planning and leaving enough room to change plans at any moment. The plan can always be improved when one reaches the destination. Travel plans should not be too rigid, nor should we be too unprepared. There should be enough space in the itinerary to allow time to explore the locals' favourite countryside areas. Experienced travellers schedule only a part of their trip and leave the rest to be explored based on their cultural experience. Some prefer longer stays at one place, so they get the freedom to restructure their entire trip. One can replan their transport, food and accommodation after reaching the destination and it gives them a true sense of knowing the place they visit. Finally, the best approach is to plan, have *tawakkul (reliance)* on Allah and rely on His guidance for help.

> ***"If Allah helps you, none can defeat you. But if He denies you help, then who else can help you? So in Allah let the believers put their trust." (Qur'an 3:160)***

- Know your 'why' of the trip. What is the purpose?
- Keep two forms of ID, pack smart and pack light.
- Familiarize yourself with the destination before you go.
- Purchase travel insurance for international travel.
- Avoid long lines by making reservations in advance.
- Connect with the concierge at your hotel in case of weather emergencies.
- Look for free days at the museum. You might find one during your time there.
- Know your rental car well. Try to rent a vehicle with which you are familiar.
- Consider visiting your local library and checking travel guidebooks on the area. Sometimes local experts write them and they are more relevant than most vlogs and blogposts on the destination.

# Staying Connected During Travel

Travelling is an excellent way to find rejuvenation. It brings us outside our comfort zones and makes meaningful memories for us. However, for Muslims, any type of travel is incomplete or even counterproductive, if it takes us away from the remembrance of Allah. Islam is a way of life that introduces human beings to their essence, the soul. The only way for our soul to revive itself is by remembering the One who created it. As Muslims, we must stay connected with the Almighty, just as He is in touch with every minute of our existence.

# Travel with *Taqwā*

*"O believers! Be mindful of Allah in the way He deserves and do not die except in a state of full submission to Him."* (Qur'an 3:102)

Islam provides us with a moderate and flexible way of living. Our Prophet ﷺ displayed that in his entire life. The teachings of this *deen* (way of life) are not meant to impose strict rules upon us, but rather to guide us towards obtaining inner contentment while pursuing our worldly objectives. There is moderation in knowledge as well as actions. If we make our lives too rigid, it may become overwhelming. If we lose sight of our goals, it may lead us astray. Therefore, Islam advocates for a balanced approach in every aspect of life, including travel.

Whether we travel to see the world or embark on the path of life, there is one essential requirement for a memorable, prosperous journey and that is *taqwā*. *Taqwā* is often translated by scholars of the past as "fear of Allah." However, *taqwā* does not mean fear in its literal sense. There is an Arabic word for fear, *khawf*, which is mentioned in the Qur'an. *Taqwā* means to shield oneself from sins, to protect oneself from anything that may displease Allah. It is to fulfill the promise we have with Allah, out of love and respect for His blessings, so that we do not cross the limits and remain vigilant about not crossing the boundaries. It is to guard oneself from Allah's anger out of reverence and not be ungrateful for the countless blessings He has bestowed upon us. It is to follow in the footsteps of the Prophet ﷺ, who is known as the Imam of the *Muttaqeen* (God-conscious people). He always remained in a state of *taqwā*, as Aishah narrated, "The Prophet ﷺ used to remember Allah in all his matters."

To travel with *taqwā* means that we explore the beautiful world of Allah with the consciousness to guard ourselves from committing sins that are widespread in modern-day travelling. It means that we stay alert that Allah is watching us wherever we are. He is aware of what we think and what we plan, our actions as well as our intentions. Our life in this world is a journey and everything here is for our use, but we are for *Ākhirah*. That is our final destination. The journey becomes beautiful when we have a divine relationship with Allah and that is *taqwā*. Although we can never fully fulfill the rights of *taqwā* as ordinary humans, we should always strive to achieve it to the best of our abilities, as Allah says in the Qur'an:

***"So be mindful of Allah to the best of your ability, hear and obey and spend in charity – that will be best for you. And whoever is saved from selfishness of their own souls, it is they who are truly successful." (Qur'an 64:16)***

## The Power of Du'ā'

*"Call upon Me, I will respond to you."* (Qur'an 40:60)

Travelling can be one of the best times to make *du'ā'* (supplication). A traveller, away from home and its comforts, is a vulnerable member of society. That is why it is recommended to make supplications before one leaves for a journey and also make plenty of *du'ā'* while travelling. According to one hadith, the Prophet ﷺ said, "Three supplications are answered without a doubt: the supplication of an oppressed person, the supplication of a traveller and the supplication of a father for his child" (Tirmidhi 1905). We must also remember our friends, family members and deceased relatives in our supplications.

A traveller is also recommended to recite the *sunnah* supplication before embarking on a journey. Ibn Umar reported: When the Prophet ﷺ mounted his camel to set out on a journey, he glorified Allah ﷻ (saying Allahu Akbar) three times and then said:

*"Glory be to Him who has made this subservient to us, for we have no power over it ourselves and to our Lord we shall return"* (Qur'an 43:14).

"O Allah, we ask You during this journey for righteousness, piety and the act which pleases You. O Allah, make this journey easy for us and make the distance short for us. O Allah, You are our companion during the journey and the guardian of (our) family. O Allah, I seek refuge in You from the hardships of the journey, the gloominess of the sights and finding evil changes in property and family on return." When the Prophet ﷺ returned, he would say these words and add to them, "We are returning, repentant, worshipping our Lord and praising Him" (Muslim 1342). The Prophet ﷺ also said, "When anyone of you wishes to travel, he should pray for his friends because Allah gives good to them on account of his prayer."

Making decisions about travel can be difficult, especially when faced with two options and feeling uncertain about which to choose. In these situations, the prayer of *istikhara* can provide guidance. *Istikhara*, which means "seeking guidance from Allah," is a highly recommended prayer for decision-making. After performing the prayer, it is important to trust in Allah's plan and move forward with the chosen decision. As Muslims, it is important to include *istikhara* in our decision-making process. The Prophet ﷺ frequently practiced *istikhara* in his own life.

It was narrated by Jabir ibn Abdullah that the Prophet ﷺ said, "If anyone of you intends to do something, he should offer a two-*rak'ah* prayer other than the mandatory prayers and after finishing it, he should say, 'O Allah, I consult You, for You have all knowledge and appeal to You to support me with your Power and ask for Your Bounty, for You are able to do things while I am not and You know while I do not; and You are the Knower of the Unseen. O Allah, if You know this matter [name your matter] is good for me both at present and in the future (or in my religion), in my present life and the Hereafter, then fulfill it for me and make it easy for me and then bestow Your blessings on me in that matter. O Allah, if You know that this matter is not good for me in my religion, in my present life and in my Hereafter (or at present or in the future), then divert me from it and choose for me what is good, whatever it may be and make me be pleased with it" (Bukhari 7390).

## Planning Around *Salah*

*"Surely, Salah is an obligation on the believers that is tied up with time."* (Qur'an 4:103)

For a Muslim, there are no restrictions in travelling the world and seeing the wonders created by Allah ﷻ. However, what sets us apart from the rest of the world is our ritual prayer, *salah*. The five mandatory prayers not only must be performed on time (with exceptions during travel) but also serve as a way to remember Allah ﷻ and revive our connection with Him. During *salah*, we communicate with Allah through the Qur'an, supplications and by submitting ourselves in prostration. It is an act of gratitude that reminds us of the favours bestowed upon us by Allah. *Salah* is an opportunity to disconnect from the world and focus on the Almighty. It is a mindfulness technique that refreshes the body and mind. As Muslims, we must plan our lives around *salah*, as it will be the first question we will be asked about in *Ākhirah* (Hereafter).

The five mandatory *salah* must never be missed, even when travelling. Therefore, planning the trip around the prayer times must be learned. Starting from the flight booking, it is best to choose the time after *Fajr* (dawn prayer), so one reaches the destination by *dhuhr* (noon prayer) time. Similarly, the rest of the travel plan can be enjoyed between the prayer times. Planning around *salah* gives an additional advantage of setting small deadlines during travel. For example, one may go hiking before *dhuhr*, visit a museum between *dhuhr* and *asr* (mid-afternoon prayer), have dinner soon after *maghrib* (after sunset prayer) and so on.

## Praying at the Airport

"The whole earth has been made a sacred and pure mosque for me, so whenever the time of prayer comes for anyone of you, he should pray wherever he is." (Muslim, no. 521)

In more recent times, we have seen major city airports in Europe and North America setting aside mosques and spirituality rooms, but this is still less common in smaller airports or remote areas in the West. In such a situation, one can use available airline counters, basement lounges or the back corners of airport restaurants where the crowd is often minimal. Another alternative is to ask airport staff to locate a quiet place or a multi-faith spiritual room. In case one is unable to find a place to pray, then the best option is to make *wudu* (ablution) and ask Allah ﷻ to guide us towards it. This option, *insha'Allah* (If Allah wills), always works out. When we make a sincere intention to pray and then make an effort by doing *wudu*, Allah ﷻ makes a way for us.

Additionally, it is also essential to remember to bring a travel prayer mat. Nowadays they often come with a built-in compass to guide us towards the *qiblah* (direction of prayer, i.e. Makkah).

## Opportunity for *Sadaqa Jāriyā*

*Sadaqah Jariyah* is a continuous charity that results in rewards even after the temporary phase of life is over. The best *sadaqah jariyah* is to leave behind a righteous child who benefits parents through prayers and good deeds. However, there are many other ways to earn continuous rewards, including building a mosque, constructing a well, spreading knowledge that benefits others and leaving behind any other beneficial legacy. As a Muslim, it is important to always look for ways to leave *sadaqah jariyah* whenever possible. Travelling can help us in this area too. For instance, many airport prayer rooms have a designated area for Muslims, which is equipped with prayer mats, copies of the Qur'an and other reading materials. This could be an excellent opportunity to place dawah materials on Islam, prayer mats, rosaries or copies of the Qur'an. By doing so, anyone who benefits from these materials in the future will help pave the way for us to receive the same rewards. The Prophet ﷺ said, "Whoever guides someone to a good deed will be rewarded equally to the person who actually carried out that good deed" (Riyad as-Salihin 173).

***"Let there be a group among you who call others to goodness, encourage what is good and forbid what is evil – it is they who will be successful." (Qur'an 3:104)***

## *Wudu* and *Tayammum*

"When a person performs ablution and washes his hands, his sins exit through his hands. When he washes his face, his sins exit through his face. When he washes his forearms and wipes his head, his sins exit through his forearms and head. When he washes his feet, his sins exit through his feet." (Ibn Majah 283)

*Wudu* has a deeper significance beyond physical purification. It is a profound spiritual practice that not only refreshes the body but also the soul. As you perform each step of *wudu*, including rinsing your mouth and nose, washing the face, arms, feet and wiping over the head, you are not merely cleansing the body but also washing away minor sins, purifying the spirit and preparing for a sacred connection with Allah.

During travel, Muslims sometimes feel hesitant to perform *wudu* in shared bathrooms. Public toilets, especially at airports, are often crowded with long queues. For Muslims, it can be uncomfortable to perform the washing ritual in front of others. Regardless, we must not shy away from performing *wudu* for the prayer. Instead, the focus must be on the mandatory acts of *wudu*, which include washing the face and arms (up to the elbows), wiping the head and washing the feet (up to the ankles). If *wudu* was done before putting on socks, one could wipe over the socks when refreshing *wudu* the next time, as long as the socks were not removed in between. This is valid for up to three days and three nights for travellers.[1] The socks must be up to or above the ankles and not sheer or torn. Some scholars recommend only wiping over leather socks, while others say it applies to all types of socks.

As Muslims, it is important to be mindful of our water usage and cleanliness. Leaving the toilet or sink area wet can reflect poorly on our ablution and Islamic practices in general. Therefore, it is crucial to wipe dry the area after use.

In situations where water is unavailable, *tayammum* is an alternative method of ablution. This dry ablution method is explained in the Qur'an and involves using clean earth to wipe the face and hands. It can be performed in cases such as illness, travelling, open wounds, extreme cold or when sufficient water is not available within a one-mile radius. Tayammum sets are now available in the market, but if not, one may use clean sand, stone, limestone or clay for this purpose. It's important to note that materials such as wood, glass, metal or paper cannot be used for *Tayammum.*[2]

*"If you are ill, on a journey or have relieved yourselves or been intimate with your wives and cannot find water, then purify yourselves with clean earth, wiping your face and hands. And Allah is Ever-Pardoning, All-Forgiving."* (Qur'an 4:43)

## *Qasr*, the Shortened Travel Prayer

*"When you travel through the land, it is permissible for you to shorten the prayer."* (Qur'an 4:101)

As Muslims, it is important for us to understand the principles of *qasr*, which is the prayer of the traveller. This prayer becomes valid when we are at least forty-eight miles away from home (based on the distance a camel can cover in three days).[3] When praying *qasr*, the four-*rak'ah fard* (obligatory) prayers of *dhuhr*, *asr* and *isha* (nightfall) become two *rak'ah*, while the rest of the prayers remain the same. The Prophet ﷺ and his companions performed the prayer of *qasr*. Anas narrated that the Prophet ﷺ said, "Allah has waived half of the prayer and fasting for the traveller and for pregnant women and the sick" (an-Nasai 2274).

With regards to combining the prayers, there is a difference of opinion among scholars. While some suggest combining *dhuhr* and *asr* prayers and maghrib and *isha* prayers, others recommend praying *dhuhr* in the later half and *asr* in its earliest start time. Allah ﷻ knows best. We can no longer shorten the prayer once we are back in our home city.

Ibn Abbas narrated, "The Prophet ﷺ once stayed for nineteen days and prayed shortened prayers. So, when we travelled and stayed for nineteen days, we used to shorten the prayer and if we travelled (and stayed) for a longer period we used to offer the full prayer." (Bukhari 1080)

Paying *qasr* in a moving vehicle is also not uncommon. Here are some points to consider, recommended by scholars.

If one is in a moving vehicle during the obligatory prayer time and it is likely that the prayer time will be over before reaching the destination and the prayer can also not be combined (like *Fajr* or *isha*), one must pray during the journey. If a person can stop at a nearby mosque or any other point like a petrol station (such as during a road trip), then one must offer the prayer in the conventional way.

When the direction of the *qiblah* can be determined, such as on a boat or train and there is space to stand up, then you must pray the conventional way. But if the direction of the *qiblah* and the place to stand are both unavailable, then we just pray the best we can and the direction of the moving vehicle, such as an airplane or a bus, becomes the direction of our prayer.

## Protection from Neglect

*"So be mindful of Allah to the best of your ability, hear and obey and spend in charity – that will be best for you. And whoever is saved from the selfishness of their own souls, it is they who are truly successful."* (Qur'an 64:16)

A typical day of travel in the modern world may seem like a succession of scheduled events, from praying *Fajr* to rushing to the airport, checking baggage, passing security, waiting in the lounge, boarding the plane and picking up a rental car. Consequently, it is easy to be consumed by worldly thoughts as one moves from one place to another. One may feel sinful for being in a state of *ghaflah* (ignorance), given that the entire day was spent packing, driving and flying. What can protect us from a state of neglect during a busy day of travel is through *dhikr*. Allah's *dhikr* does not rely on whether or not one has *wudu*, nor does it require a specific time to perform. It can be done anywhere, at any time.

*Dhikr* (remembrance) is a means of spiritual elevation. It redirects our attention to nourishing our souls and refreshing our minds. The person who remembers Allah ﷻ is under His protection and is prayed for by the angels. The tongue, moistened by the *dhikr* of Allah ﷻ, is safeguarded against lying and backbiting. The eyes and ears are protected against sins and the roots of *iman* find strength. One can perform any type of *dhikr*, such as *subhanAllah*, *alhamdulillah*, *Allahu Akbar* or *subhanAllahi wa bihamdihi* or even a simple *istighfar* by saying *astaghfir-ullah* while walking long distances at the airport, waiting to board the plane or sitting on the flight. Carrying a *misbaha* (prayer beads), especially one with thirty-three beads or wearing a *tasbih* bracelet, can serve as a friendly reminder for *dhikr*.

***"Surely in the remembrance of Allah do hearts find comfort." (Qur'an 13:28)***

Travelling often involves waiting, whether it is for security checks, boarding a mode of transportation or reaching the destination. It may range from a few minutes to several hours, depending on the distance of the travel. While waiting, people often engage in various activities like checking social media, watching movies, sleeping or striking up a conversation with fellow travellers. However, it is also an excellent opportunity to do something meaningful such as memorizing *du'ā'* from the Qur'an and *sunnah*.

There are many supplications that we find helpful and want to memorize, but the demands of our daily routine often make it difficult. However, we can effectively use our waiting time to memorize important supplications that require understanding and memorization. One such supplication is "Sayyid *al-Istighfar*," the master *dhikr* of *tawbah* (repentance). The Prophet ﷺ said, "The most superior way of asking forgiveness from Allah is:

"اللَّهُمَّ أَنْتَ رَبِّي لاَ إِلَهَ إِلَّا أَنْتَ، خَلَقْتَنِي وَأَنَا عَبْدُكَ، وَأَنَا عَلَى عَهْدِكَ وَوَعْدِكَ مَا اسْتَطَعْتُ، أَعُوذُ بِكَ مِنْ شَرِّ مَا صَنَعْتُ، أَبُوءُ لَكَ بِنِعْمَتِكَ عَلَيَّ، وَأَبُوءُ لَكَ بِذَنْبِي فَاغْفِرْ لِي، فَإِنَّهُ لاَ يَغْفِرُ الذُّنُوبَ إِلَّا أَنْتَ."

'O Allah, You are my Lord. None has the right to be worshipped but You. You created me and I am your slave and I am faithful to my covenant and my promise as much as I can. I seek refuge with You from all the evil

I have done. I acknowledge before You all the blessings You have bestowed upon me and I confess to You all my sins. So, forgive me, for nobody can forgive sins except You.'"

The Prophet ﷺ then added, "If somebody recites it during the day with firm faith in it and dies on the same day before the evening, he will be from the people of Paradise; and if somebody recites it at night with firm faith in it and dies before the morning, he will be from the people of Paradise" (Bukhari 6306).

Imagine being on a regular flight where others may be occupied with worldly matters, but we utilize this time to learn something new that can contribute to our success in *Ākhirah*. We can use this opportunity to learn supplications mentioned in the Qur'an or hadith.

## Enjoining Unity

*"Thus have We made of you an Ummah (community of believers) just balanced."* (Qur'an 2:143)

Muslims are united through their belief in Allah ﷻ and the Prophet ﷺ, regardless of their language or ethnicity. As the *ummah* of the last Prophet ﷺ, we share a common bond of brotherhood (or sisterhood) and have an intrinsic attachment to mosques. When we travel, we have an excellent opportunity to follow the example of the Prophet's ﷺ companions by meeting with other Muslims and joining their communities. One way to do it is to find mosques wherever we go. By visiting new mosques, we get an opportunity to meet warm and kind-hearted Muslims who are also striving for success in *Ākhirah*. Sometimes, we get invited to dinners with beautiful families and their generosity and hospitality may lead to lifelong friendships. Moreover, socializing allows us to spread *salaam* (peace), as the Prophet ﷺ said,

"Verily, the best people to Allah are those who are first to greet with peace" (Abu Dawud 5197).

*Alhamdulillah*, Islam is spreading rapidly in the West and a small Islamic center can be found in most tourist areas. One may avail of this opportunity by asking the managing team at the mosque about their needs. At times, smaller Islamic centers are in need of assistance, such as financial aid for a pending project or the need for more materials for their Islamic school or dawah purposes. We can visit the mosque and tour the area. Afterward, we can keep in touch and continue supporting them through donations, a spiritually rewarding way to earn *sadaqah jariyah*. Additionally, we can earn extra rewards by praying two *rak'ahs* at the mosque, as advised by Prophet ﷺ: "When one of you enters the mosque, let him not sit down until he has prayed two *rak'ahs*" (Bukhari 1167).

***"O Mankind, We have created you from a male and a female and made you into races and tribes, so that you may identify one another. Surely the noblest of you, in Allah's sight, is the one who is most pious of you. Surely, Allah is All-Knowing, All-Aware." (Qur'an 49:13)***

## Representing Deen

Abu Darda reported that the Prophet ﷺ said, "Nothing is heavier upon the scale of a believer on the Day of Resurrection than good character." (Tirmidhi 2002)

As Muslims, we represent our *deen* wherever we go. We are obligated to learn the teachings of Islam, spread it to others and invite them to the message of *tawhid* (the Oneness of Allah). Travelling provides an excellent opportunity to do so, especially when visiting countries with a non-Muslim majority. Islam encourages us to greet others with a friendly smile and we must always remember the importance of being good neighbours to those around us, including fellow travellers on buses or trains. One must recall that Islam spread through the good character of Muslim traders and not by the sword. People were drawn to Islam because of its simple message of monotheism, strong morality and ethics. The early Muslims who travelled across the globe invited others to Islam through their good conduct. Their acts of courtesy left a lasting positive impression of Muslims. Therefore, when there is an opportunity to talk about Islam, the hijab or *salah*, we must respond to others with the best of manners because we are the *ummah* (nation) of the Prophet, who sets an example for the best manners and character.

*"And verily, you (O Muhammad) are on an exalted (standard of) character."* (Qur'an 68:4)

## Travel Conversations

*"And of the people is he who buys the amusement of speech to mislead (others) from the way of Allah without knowledge and who takes it (his way) in ridicule. Those will have a humiliating punishment."* (Qur'an 31:6)

Oftentimes, we overhear people talking aloud when travelling by airplane, bus or train. The conversations can be an empathetic talk with a stranger who lost a loved one or exchange of ideas about one's current projects. People may also have a productive discussion about their hometown and share ideas on community-building and restorations. These types of conversations are mostly positive and amicable. However, negative talks, such as boasting about one's achievements or complaining about one's life, may also happen. We might also get drawn into conversations about our material possessions, high-ranking jobs or travelling swag, all of which may represent unhealthy materialism. Such ostentatious dialogues were not the way of our Prophet ﷺ or his companions. Useless conversations are loved by the base self and may lead us to lie, gossip and show off, which are considered sins. Over-sharing personal information can also become a target of the evil eye and stir jealousy in others against us. Therefore, we must avoid excessive talking and limit our conversations to polite exchanges.

Ibn Umar narrated that the Prophet ﷺ said, "Do not talk too much without remembrance of Allah. Indeed, excessive talking without remembering Allah hardens the heart. And indeed, the farthest of people from Allah is the harsh-hearted." (Tirmidhi 2411)

## Not Compromising Our Principles

"There are two types of dwellers of Hell whom I did not see (in my time): people having flogs like tails of ox and with them they would be beating people and women who would be dressed but appear to be naked." (Muslim 2128)

As Muslims, we follow gender-specific rules for clothing called *satr,* which defines our identity as Muslims, especially in public. We must make sure that our public attire is not too tight, sheer or revealing. However, it is not uncommon to see Muslims changing their dress code when on vacation. Unfortunately, it is more noticeable with women, who may remove the hijab or wear brighter outfits when travelling out of town or engaging in outdoor activities such as hiking. Men too need to dress according to Islamic guidelines for them, such as avoiding wearing anything that may expose the thighs. It is crucial to note that there is no connection between clothing style and physical activity, other than following trends. Rather, wearing loose-fitted clothes on a summer hike can protect against harmful sun rays and mosquitoes. Moreover, we must remember that even when on vacation, our angels are still watching us and we must dress modestly and avoid ostentation as recommended by Islam. Our clothes reflect our Muslim identity and both men and women must portray that honourably in public.

"Whoever believes in Allah and the Last Day, let him not sit at a table where wine is being served." (Tirmidhi 2801)

*"They ask you about wine and gambling. Say, 'In both there is great sin and some benefits for people. And their sin is greater than their benefit.'" (Qur'an 2:219)*

As a Muslim, it is important to be mindful of the places we visit during our vacations. It is advised to avoid areas such as wineries, taprooms and casinos, as they go against the standards set by our *iman*. It is beneath the caliber of a Muslim to be at a place where there is gambling, alcohol and nudity. However, if there is no other option for food, then one may take the food to-go and walk out immediately.

Similarly, when visiting beaches in non-Muslim countries, it is important to be mindful of the time of day. Beaches are no doubt beautiful and one must go to enjoy the beauty of water. However, we can go to the beach earlier in the day: morning hours are best for exploring the beach as the crowd is minimal and our eyes are protected from committing sins. (On a side note, photos of the beach are better in the morning light.)

In essence, our bucket list too should remind us of Allah ﷾. We must avoid visiting any place that may displease Allah ﷾.

# The Barakah Hours

Abu Hurairah narrated that the Prophet ﷺ said, "Do as many good deeds as you can. The best deeds are those done regularly, even if they are few in number." (Ibn Majah 4240)

An airplane may fly for hours, but eventually it must land on the ground to get refueled. Likewise, humans need to refuel their souls every few hours with *dhikr* and *salah*. The most important time for this refueling is early in the morning, at dawn or pre-dawn. This is when we sit quietly and get involved in the *dhikr* of Allah, who gives us a chance to rectify our matters for the Hereafter. Our daily rituals of *dhikr* beautifully connect our worldly life and our faith.

Unfortunately, our routine of *dhikr* may be disrupted while travelling and we may find it difficult to find time for it. We should remind ourselves that travelling must not separate us from *Ākhirah*. The special bond with Allah ﷻ must not weaken during our vacation. Similarly, it is beneficial to continue the habit of reading the Qur'an after *Fajr* if one does it regularly at home.

*"Can (such people be equal to) the one who worships during the hours of night, prostrating himself and standing, fearing the Hereafter and having hopes in his Lord's mercy? Say, 'Can those who know*

*and those who do not know become equal?' It is only the people of understanding who are receptive of the advice."* (Qur'an 39:9)

Travel may also help us develop a new habit of early morning *dhikr*. As people are free from the monotony of daily routine, they may find extra time in the morning to develop a habit of doing the *dhikr* of Allah. Even just the *dhikr* of *alhamdulillah* and *laa ilaha illallah* each morning, when performed repeatedly, can add enormous rewards into our account. *Dhikr* of Allah makes us morally and emotionally strong, brings the shine of divine light on the face and nourishes the soul. Ultimately, the source of strength comes only through our connection with Allah.

> ***"The best remembrance is laa ilaha ilallah and the best supplication is alhamdulillah." (Tirmidhi 3383)***

Instead of sleeping in and disrupting our body's natural rhythm, a traveller can maintain their regular sleep-wake cycle and take advantage of the morning hours. The first four hours after *Fajr* are particularly productive for Muslims, as the Prophet ﷺ prayed for blessings for his *ummah* during this time. While it may be tempting to stay up late uploading photos or editing videos, a wise traveller prioritizes the morning hours and avoids compromising them for sleep. Experienced travellers wake up early, have a healthy breakfast and start their day with a morning hike or other planned activities, such as visiting a museum or going on a sightseeing tour.

"O Allah, bless my nation in their early morning." (Tirmidhi 1212)

## Travel for Knowledge

Abu Darda narrated that Prophet Muhammad ﷺ said, "If anyone travels in search of knowledge, Allah will guide them to one of the paths of Paradise. The angels will be pleased with those who seek knowledge and will spread their wings over them. The dwellers of the heavens and the Earth, even the fish in the depths of the water, will ask Allah for forgiveness on behalf of the knowledgeable person. The superiority of a knowledgeable person over a devout person is like the superiority of a full moon over the rest of the stars." (Abu Dawud 3641)

Islam encourages Muslims to explore and learn about the world around them and to reflect on Allah's ﷻ creations. By visiting new places, meeting people from different backgrounds and hearing their languages, we can gain a deeper understanding of the world and its inhabitants. Travelling and learning new things is an auspicious way to strengthen our faith and become better individuals. When we look at the Islamic scholars of the past, we see that they had a great thirst for knowledge and were willing to travel long distances to acquire it. They set examples of selflessness and humility, such as Imam Bukhari, who endured poverty and ate modest food while collecting hadiths in far-off lands. Their dedication to knowledge strengthened their faith and improved their character.

***"And for who have adopted the right path, Allah improves them in guidance and gives them their piety." (Qur'an 47:17)***

Travelling is considered a form of knowledge. It must be beneficial for both the traveller and others or else it could lead to ignorance and failure. It should broaden our minds, provide reasoning and wisdom and help us understand the One who created us. Islamic history is enriched with examples of travelling scholars and historical landmarks. One can visit Fez to see the al-Qarawiyyin University, the first university in the world founded by a Muslim woman, Fatima al-Fihri or travel to Granada to see remnants of Muslim Spain. Similarly, one can travel to learn about the spread of Islam across the world, such as in China, where the Great Mosque of Xian can be found. In the past, Muslim travellers would also read about natural wonders and then travel to see them. For example, they would contemplate on the Qur'anic verse about the mixing of waters and then search for places to see it: "He merges the two bodies of (fresh and salt) water, yet between them is a barrier they never cross" (Qur'an 59:19).

Travelling to explore beautiful landscapes and learning about their geology and topography enlightens us with the magnificence of Allah ﷾. Travelling expands our knowledge and understanding beyond what we learn at school. True happiness comes from spiritual enlightenment and knowledge is the light that guides us towards it. Having a mind that is blessed with a large storage of knowledge and the ability to contemplate the reasoning behind things is a blessing from Allah ﷾.

> ***"And He placed mountains on the earth, lest it should shake with you and rivers and tracks, so that you may find the right way and He has set landmarks. And by the stars they find the right way." (Qur'an 16:15-16)***

## Returning Belongings

*"O my people! This worldly life is only (a fleeting) enjoyment, whereas the Hereafter is truly a home of settlement."* (Qur'an 40:39)

The modern world of social media portrays this world as a permanent abode. Our constant desire for more material possessions and belongings often leads us to lose the battle with our *nafs* (propensity). Travelling, on the other hand, can help us reconnect with our inner soul and provide a much-needed reality check. When we travel, we can only pack a few essential items and leave our homes and other belongings behind. This experience can serve as a metaphor for our afterlife, where we will only carry what matters most: our virtuous deeds.

Moreover, travelling also helps us understand the unpredictability of life, as one may not be able to return from the journey. Therefore, scholars recommend that we should return any borrowed items before going on a trip. We have the example of our Prophet ﷺ whom the people of Makkah trusted for their assets. The Prophet ﷺ asked Ali رضي الله عنه to safely return the pledges entrusted to him by the people of Makkah.

Likewise, if the head of a family is going on a trip, he must leave enough funds with his family and allocate resources to seek help in case of emergencies. Additionally, the family must bid farewell to the one who is travelling. Once, a man came to the Prophet ﷺ and said, "I intend to go on a travel, so give me some advice." The Prophet ﷺ said to him, "In the protection and care of Allah. May Allah supply you with piety, pardon your sins and direct you to good wherever you are" (Riyad as-Salihin 978).

## Other Travel *Sunnahs*

The principles of the Prophet ﷺ provide the best guidance in all situations, including travel. The following are some of his *sunnahs* that can be adopted to have a safe journey and uneventful homecoming.

**A leader on the journey:** The Prophet ﷺ advised choosing a leader when three or more people travel as a group. He said, "When three persons set out on a journey, they should appoint one of them as their leader" (Riyad al-Salihin 960). The reason is to avoid disagreements and find a consensus when making a decision. It is important for the group leader to be knowledgeable and trustworthy, as he will be entrusted with others' affairs.

**Returning home:** The Prophet ﷺ preferred arriving home during daylight hours after travelling, as there was no way to inform his family of the arrival time beforehand. Arriving late at night could cause problems for the family, who may not be expecting the traveller. Before going home, the Prophet ﷺ would also perform voluntary prayer at the mosque. According to Kaab ibn Malik, "The Prophet ﷺ never returned from a journey except in the mid-morning. He would start at the mosque, where he would offer a two-*rak'ah* voluntary prayer and sit for a while before going home" (Ṣaḥīḥ al-Bukhārī 2922). The Prophet ﷺ also advised his companions to present themselves well when returning home.

# Staying Healthy While Travelling

"Health is wealth" is a saying that holds true even when we are on vacation. Our wellbeing during travel is as important as where we stay and the places we visit. In this section, we will explore ways to enhance and recharge our physical, mental and spiritual health while travelling. We will look at how to eat healthily, deal with jetlag, make better food choices, stay physically active and ask the right questions when dining out. Additionally, we will see how travelling can uplift our mood and reduce anxiety and depression. We will also learn about wellness travel, a popular form of travel that focuses on improving health and wellbeing.

# Travel Diet

*"O children of Adam, take your adornment at every mosque and eat and drink, but be not excessive. Indeed, He does not like those who commit excess."* (Qur'an 7:31)

Trying new cuisines and local specialties is a significant part of travelling. Whether from a street vendor or a restaurant, food plays a vital role in our travel experiences. When we visit a new place, we often hear about a "must-try" dish recommended by locals. However, many people struggle to control the types of food they eat while travelling and some even travel specifically for food. This can lead to unhealthy eating habits, which can have long-term effects on our bodies. Those travelling with their families often feel like it is impossible to eat healthy, as children may demand unhealthy snacks like crisps and fizzy drinks. However, it's important to prioritize healthy eating, as getting sick during or after travel or developing chronic health problems later in life is not worth indulging in unhealthy foods.

Our vacations are not about abandoning a healthy lifestyle or gaining weight. The development of chronic diseases does not get halted by our travel, as unhealthy food choices harm the body whether at home or travelling. As a result, we may develop an aggravation in inflammation levels due to our vacation. Therefore, experts recommend travellers understand why a healthy diet is crucial during travel, especially in relation to our gut.

Our gut contains trillions of bacteria that form a colony called a microbiome, which plays a significant role in our immune system. What we eat interacts with our microbiome and can either promote healing or inflammation, i.e., our food decides the consequence.[1] Processed foods such as crisps, biscuits, fizzy drinks, sweets, white bread and all artificially flavoured packaged items are quickly absorbed by our digestive system, causing a sugar spike that promotes inflammation. If this cycle of rapid sugar spikes continues, it can lead to insulin resistance and obesity. Inflammation and insulin resistance caused by an unhealthy diet are the roots of all modern diseases.[2]

Allah has created our body organs very strong. When we stop consuming pro-inflammatory convenience foods, our organs start healing themselves. They are our best guides and show us symptoms when we eat something wrong. It is up to us to observe our body and its needs. Our body demands real food, anything that one can picture in its raw state or pronounce the ingredient list. We have a choice to pick a highly processed white bread loaf or choose a healthier version of whole grain wheat bread. The same principle goes with fruits, vegetables, nuts and seeds.

Adhering to simple eating habits is the key to staying healthy during travel and elsewhere. This was the preferred style of our Prophet ﷺ, who followed a very healthy approach to his diet and overall lifestyle.

*"O mankind, eat from whatever is on earth (that is) lawful and pure and do not follow the footsteps of Satan. Indeed, he is to you a clear enemy."* (Qur'an 2:168)

## Halal and Permissible

*"Forbidden to you (for food) are dead meat, blood, the flesh of swine and that on which has been invoked the name of other than Allah."* (Qur'an 5:3)

Nowadays, halal food options are relatively easy to find, *alhamdulillah*. One may be travelling to a location up north and be surprised to see a halal restaurant there. However, even if a halal option is available, one must still inquire about the source of the meat. The restaurant caterers are often kind enough to tell us where they get their *zabihah* meat from.

Sometimes, we may be travelling to a specific location with no Muslim population or halal eatery nearby. This is especially relatable near national or provincial parks, which are often in rural areas and halal food is rarely available in the vicinity. In such a case, we have a few choices.

**Seafood:** It is always one of the safest options for a Muslim when halal meat is not available. Fish do not have a requirement of *zabiha* (halal slaughter), nor a rule that it must only be cut by a Muslim. Despite that, a few points must be kept in mind. Firstly, choose wild seafood options to avoid consuming cancer-causing industrial chemicals that contaminate seafood. Secondly, ask about cross-contamination of fish with other meat types, such as during grilling or frying. If the restaurant has only one grill, we may ask them to wrap our food in foil to avoid contact with haram meat. Additionally, it is important to ask about fish batter when ordering fried fish, as beer batter is commonly used, especially in the coastal areas of the West.

**Traditional cuisines:** African cuisines, such as those from Morocco, Tunisia or Ethiopia, are also good options when halal food is not available. Authentic African food is known for its rich taste and fresh ingredients and the menu may include legume-based dishes, harira, injera and so on. Mediterranean food is another healthier choice and one can order falafel or a platter with pita bread, olives, cheese and sauce. However, it is important to inquire about cross-contamination when ordering fried vegetarian items or bread, as they may be fried or baked with meat. Furthermore, Asian cuisines, like the ones from Pakistan and India, offer many delicious vegetarian options. Here, too, one must inquire about cross-contamination, such as if the bread rolls are made in the same pan as the meat.

**Vegan and vegetarian:** These, too, are safe options. However, one must be careful about the condiments as wine-based sauces are commonly used nowadays. While red wine vinegar is considered halal by many Islamic scholars, one must still inquire about the salad dressing ingredients to avoid the use of alcohol. Additionally, servers must change their gloves even when preparing salads.

As Muslims, we should not feel hesitant to discuss our dietary requirements with the servers. Most restaurants appreciate customers who specify their meal preferences and religious dietary requirements. Eating halal and *tayyib* (pure) food is a mandatory responsibility, as we shall be asked what we eat and drink. Abu Hurairah narrated that the Prophet ﷺ said, "Verily, the first thing a servant will be asked about on the Day of Resurrection will be his blessings. It will be said to him, 'Have We not given you health in your body and nourished you with cool water to drink?'" (Tirmidhi 3358).

*"Eat and drink of that which Allah has provided and do not act corruptly, making mischief on earth."* (Qur'an 2:60)

## Road Trips

Travelling by road is one of the best ways to experience the outdoors. It gives a level of independence to travellers who may continue their journey and stop whenever they are tired. However, if not planned correctly, our road trips may end up detrimental for our health. One may stop at a petrol station and grab a bag full of packaged pastries, fizzy drinks and other convenient food items, all contributing to higher blood sugar and cholesterol levels.[3] Our road trips can turn into days of fast food, diner orders and rest-stop processed meals if we do not plan ahead. Consequently, we may return from our road trip feeling sluggish and exhausted.

It is possible to stay healthy during road trips.[4] Some of the easy, practical and affordable tips for maintaining a healthy lifestyle while travelling by road include:

1. Have a food pack ready. It is helpful to bring a cooler in the backseat where one may keep one's favourite snacks. The food pack should include nuts like almonds, macadamia and pecans and seeds like pumpkin and sunflower seeds. We can also include foods high in healthy fats, such as canned wild salmon or halal beef jerky. Foods that are high in healthy fats are satiating and can help prevent one

from reaching out for unhealthy options. We should also have some fresh items like hard-boiled eggs, baby carrots, cucumbers, avocados and celery. We can also pack some nut butter, hummus and tahini in our travel tiffin.

2. When our travel schedule is hectic and there is no time or space for snacks, the petrol station is often the only option left. In such a case, we must choose the healthiest version from the choices available. One may scan the aisles for heathier items like fresh apples oranges and bananas. We can also pick a stash of nuts, unflavoured Greek yogurt or a hummus dip with pita bread.

3. Avoid granola bars and trail mixes. They sound healthy but often contain inflammation-causing ingredients including corn syrup, artificial flavours and refined oils. If one needs to choose a snack bar, experts suggest using whole grains, nuts or dried fruits as main ingredients rather than refined grains and sugar. As a rule, choose the one with at least one gram of fiber for every ten grams of carbohydrate, known as the 10:1 ratio rule.

4. A bottle of water is a must. It is essential to carry a bottle of water and keep ourselves well hydrated on a road trip to avoid binging on processed snacks

and salt cravings. It is better to go for plain or detox water (with a slice of lemon, cucumber and a few mint leaves). Avoid sugary drinks and mineral supplement drops.

The easiest and most economical option is to visit the local grocery store during stops. We may not only find healthier snacks but also some freshly baked artisan bread such as sourdough or focaccia.

## At the Airport and In-Flight

It is often said that it is difficult to eat healthily when travelling by air. The rush at the airport, restrictions on certain foods during the flight and high prices at airport restaurants are some of the reasons why it seems impossible to eat well. However, with some pre-planning, we can still enjoy a healthy air journey. Here are some tips that can help.

Prepare before leaving. Bringing our own healthy snacks and meals from home is always a good idea. It saves money and also serves as an emergency food pack in case we do not have time to purchase food at the airport or if the flight does not offer permissible options. We can pack fresh fruits, nuts, cheese sticks, hummus and pita and even homemade sandwiches. Travellers from the past never left their homes without packing food.

Instead, meal planning during travel was an important aspect of their journey.

Scan the airport terminal and its food options to find healthier meal choices. We can also do a quick online search for halal options at the airport, especially if travelling in the West. We might be surprised to find a locally produced halal food cart nearby. If we have time, we can also walk to other terminals, such as the international terminals, to find more dietary choices.

When flying, it's a good idea to bring our own food from home. If that is not possible, the airport is the next best option. If halal is unavailable, one may opt for vegan food choices. Vegan meals are often made from locally sourced fruits and vegetables and are lighter on the stomach, which can help prevent bloating and fatigue during the flight.

Staying hydrated when flying is important as the pressurized cabin and recirculated air can cause dehydration. Although you may want to drink less water to avoid using the restroom, maintaining good hydration levels is crucial to staying energized and having proper digestive functioning. This will also help prevent air travel fatigue and jetlag.

## At Our Travel Destination

Upon reaching our travel destination, we may encounter two common scenarios, either reaching too late and not finding many options available or being very tired from travel and eating junk food out of convenience. To avoid this, it is important to consider the following points:

- Look for buffet options. It is a good idea to do some quick research before choosing where to eat. Buffets can offer a variety of options but try not to try everything available. Instead, scan the options first and then make a choice.

- Search for local grocery stores near the hotel or Airbnb. One may find freshly prepared salads and deli options here (if halal options are available). Similarly, one can make a list of halal or other healthy restaurants to check out before heading to the destination. It saves time and energy that one may waste looking for a restaurant upon reaching the destination.

- For breakfast, it is recommended to start with a piece of fruit like an apple or an orange, along with a detox drink such as lemon water if it's available. This provides an early morning fiber boost to aid digestion while preparing our gut for the upcoming breakfast meal. It's worth noting that our Prophet ﷺ also preferred fruits and lighter meals. In fact, a narration from Sahl ibn Sa'd states, "The Prophet ﷺ used to eat dates with melon" (Ibn Majah 3326).

- If one prefers the continental breakfast at a hotel, then it's recommended to make healthier choices, like choosing wheat bread over white bread and avoiding sugary cereals and deep-fried meat. Another good option for breakfast is to find a family-owned restaurant and dine there. The food is prepared fresh and we get to meet with the locals, who are often welcoming and hospitable.

- A heavy breakfast is preferred if a long hike is planned for the day. Otherwise, a lighter meal might be preferred if the day involves strolling around the main street for shopping. Another strategy is to have two meals per day, including breakfast and an early dinner, followed by a post-dinner tea. This saves money and prevents overeating. Moreover, skipping lunch helps our body utilize the extra calories consumed from eating at restaurants. Additionally, moderate eating is also a *sunnah* of our Prophet ﷺ, who once said, "A believer eats in one intestine (satisfied with less food) and the disbeliever eats in seven intestines (eats too much)" (Ibn Majah 3256).

- One of the best options for travellers is to book accommodation with a kitchenette. This usually includes a suite room where a small kitchen with utensils is available. This can be ideal for a family vacation where preparing food in the hotel room is both fun and budget friendly.
- Other keys to eating healthy at a restaurant include skipping appetizers or sharing them (to avoid over-eating), having an entrée with fresh vegetables as a main dish, skipping salad dressings and asking for lemon and olive oil instead and sharing the dessert with others. We can also pack our entrée in a box, which not only helps with portion control but also saves money and time for the next dinner or breakfast. Lastly, a cup of green tea after eating out is helpful for a quick detoxification boost to our liver.

## Eating After a Strenuous Hike

What to eat after a strenuous hike is often a hot topic during a backpacking trip. Those who frequently go on outdoor trips often learn to choose their post-hike meals based on their body's needs. However, there are a few universal points that anyone can follow to have a better post-hike experience.

- A strenuous hike induces a rigorous cycle of burning glycogen stores in the muscles. That is why muscle recovery is critical in avoiding soreness and pain for the following weeks. One way to have a good hiking experience is to eat a nutritious meal before starting the hike. This includes a diet high in good fats and carbohydrates, such as pita bread sandwiches, eggs, meat and oatmeal. Hydration is also vital, not only during the hike but also the day before it.

- What to eat during the hike is a personal choice; however, it is important to choose the right foods to eat during a hike. One of the simplest and healthiest choices is a banana with some pecans. One may eat two or even more of this fruit during a hike to stay full and energized. Pre-cut watermelons also help with staying hydrated while trekking. Some hikers prefer vegan granola, but they are not the healthiest choices due to added sugars.

- After the hike, the type of food one eats depends on the strenuosity of the hiking track. An intense hike can be taxing on our muscles and requires a diet high in protein and carbs to prevent muscle soreness. Salmon, beef and chicken are good sources of protein. To replenish glycogen stores in your muscles, you need a high-carb boost. Foods like rice and potatoes can help. Some also like to eat bagels with cream cheese or fries after an arduous hike.

- Staying hydrated is crucial, but it is important to avoid overhydration as it can cause hyponatremia, a condition where our body's salt levels drop dangerously low. Drinking enough water makes it easier to recover after a strenuous hike. While plain water is the best option, some prefer chocolate milk to boost their energy immediately after hiking.

Our hiking meals are about replenishing glycogen stores and keeping us hydrated. The best way to do this is by eating real food and avoiding packaged foods. If only packaged food is available, learning how to read labels and choosing the healthiest option is essential.

## A Connoisseur of Food Labels

*"Say, 'Not equal are the pure and impure, although the abundance of impure might impress you.' So fear Allah, O you of understanding, that you may be successful."* (Qur'an 5:100)

While travelling, it can be challenging to avoid packaged foods. However, being mindful of how to choose food items can help us make the best choices and avoid anything that is not *tayyib*. Nutrition labels are useful in this, as they are designed to help us make healthier choices. While it is generally recommended to look at food as a whole and not break it down into protein, carbs and fats, there are times when we must differentiate based on micronutrient information to avoid unwanted ingredients. Here are five basic tips for reading a nutrition label.

- The ingredient list. As Muslim travellers, we must make sure that the food we consume does not contain any haram ingredients. Along with that, one must avoid items like fruit juice concentrate, corn syrup, dextrose and fructose, as they can cause sugar spikes in our blood, leading to inflammation, fatty liver and heart diseases. If the ingredient list seems unfamiliar and contains technical names that are hard to pronounce, it means that the food is ultra-processed and should be avoided.

- Serving size: The serving size information is essential to keep in mind. The topmost area of the label shows the serving size and if we consume more than one serving size, we may end up consuming extra calories. A serving size may not always be the recommended dietary intake for a specific food item. Instead, it represents what most people eat and drink.

- Percentage daily value: Pay attention to the percentage daily value per serving size. It is best to stay under 100 percent daily value for saturated fat, sodium and added sugars. It is recommended to avoid food items with added sugar, especially those with more than 10%.

- Fortification: When choosing packaged food items, it is important to look for fortification with vitamins such as vitamin D, folic acid and potassium, as they are good for health.
- Fiber: One must pay close attention to the amount of fiber in the packaged item. It is best to avoid anything that has no fiber in it.

Remember, the main rule remains the same no matter what the nutrition label says: choose any snack that has more fiber and less added sugar. This applies to all types of snacks, be it crackers or crisps.

## Local Specials

*"Then eat of what Allah has provided for you (which is) lawful and good. And be grateful for the favour of Allah, if it is (indeed) Him that you worship."* (Qur'an 16:114)

**Locally-owned restaurants:** Exploring a new place through its cuisine is one of the best ways to experience it. However, if one sticks to chain restaurants instead of trying out locally owned eateries, they miss out on the authentic taste of the area. To avoid this, run a quick online search for locally owned restaurants and brunch places when travelling to a new area or ask the hotel staff for recommendations. There are several benefits to choosing locally owned restaurants. Firstly, they offer a comfortable ambiance with a homely feeling and unique entrees on their menu. They can even accommodate customers' dietary preferences. Secondly, the experience can be very personal and one may even get to meet the restaurant owners. Sometimes, the stories of how the local eatery was founded are described on the menu. Thirdly, there is a stark contrast between the choice of ingredients at a family owned versus a chain restaurant. Local dining establishments often get their produce from local farmers and the freshness of it is reflected in the taste. Finally, eating at a local restaurant may not only be cost-saving, but also a healthier experience for a travelling family.

***"You have to taste a culture to understand it." - Deborah Cater***

**Farmers markets:** Farmers markets can provide a unique culinary experience on anyone›s itinerary. Local markets offer a variety of fresh and locally sourced fruits, cheeses, jams and baked goods. These markets are typically seasonal and occur weekly, usually on

Saturdays in the United States and different days of the week in other parts of the world. They also offer healthy lunch options, such as crepes or freshly made bagel sandwiches. Visiting farmers' markets is a great way to explore the local culture and encourage healthy eating habits. It's a fun activity for families and it exposes children to new and healthy food choices. When purchasing fresh produce from a farmers' market, one must check with the government or airline guidelines to look for any travel restrictions on it. For example, the island of Hawaii places restrictions on bringing agricultural produce and tropical fruits due to the risk of introducing invasive pests.

**Foraging tours:** Foraging tours are a fun and educational experience where participants go on a hike in the meadows and woods with an expert guide, gathering edibles along the way. At the end of the hike, the group can enjoy a salad or other meal made with the foraged ingredients. Forest foraging is particularly popular and participants can learn about wild edible berries, mushrooms, greens and fruits that are often overlooked. The experts leading the tour also provide information on the process of harvesting and preparing the food after foraging is complete. While foraging tours may not be widely available, they are definitely worth experiencing if the opportunity arises on your next travel adventure.

## Avoid Overeating

"A human being fills no worse vessel than his stomach. It is sufficient for a human being to eat a few mouthfuls to keep his spine straight. But if he must (fill it), then it should be one-third for food, one-third for drink and one-third for air." (Ibn Majah 3349)

Holidays can reveal our secret eating behaviours and lifestyle choices. While it is perfectly normal to enjoy new cuisines and not to worry about dieting during holidays, one must be careful not to overeat or eat out of anxiety (to satisfy the *nafs*). A mindful eating attitude (eating only when hungry) helps us keep a check on our nutritional habits and temptations. By having control over our dietary choices and being aware of their impact on our health, we can stay healthy and avoid falling prey to our uncontrolled desires.

It is common for people to overeat while travelling due to the stress and fear of not finding food when needed. In some cases, it's true, especially when travelling with family and rushing to catch a flight. This stressful situation causes our stress hormones to spike, leading to cravings for sweeter foods. To avoid this, it's helpful to search for restaurants before the trip or bring homemade food or snacks like nuts and fruits. In addition, drinking more fluids, particularly water or herbal teas, can prevent false alarms of hunger.

One strategy to manage overeating while travelling is to adopt a compensating attitude. For instance, if we indulge in a high-sugar breakfast with cinnamon rolls or croissants, we can balance out the unhealthy diet by having a light lunch with a fruit salad or a smoothie, followed by an early dinner. By doing this, we allow our body enough time to utilize calories throughout the day. Having an early dinner also gives us some time for intermittent fasting, which is beneficial for our health.

Just as we plan our vacation, it is essential to have a strategy for our eating habits, too, while on vacation.

## An Opportunity to Walk More

*"And the servants of the Most Merciful are those who walk upon earth easily and when the ignorant address them (harshly), they say (words of) peace."* (Qur'an 25:63)

Walking is one of the best ways to connect with the places we travel to. Not only is it a great way to experience the area, but scientists have also shown that walking has incredible health benefits. While our busy everyday life may give us little time to go on foot, travel provides a perfect opportunity to do so. We can walk as much as we can. Luckily, most traveller-friendly tourist destinations are walkable, allowing one to experience a variety of sightseeing just by strolling around town. Walking comes with innumerable benefits, providing a state of being in the moment, improving energy levels, muscle and joint health and creating an overall state of wellbeing.

**Avoid line travel:** One disadvantage of a road trip is that it promotes line travel, which means rushing through multiple places in one day without taking the time to connect with the local culture. It may be tourist-friendly, but it does not benefit anyone who is looking for a new perspective on things. Line travel can make the entire journey feel superficial and forgettable. Instead, consider going car-free at times. This will not only create better memories of the trip but will also allow one to step out of the comfort zone and have new experiences.

**Prioritize walking:** It is highly recommended to prioritize walking, especially after a large meal like a heavy breakfast. One may choose to go for a walk while sightseeing or opt for a short hike. Unfortunately, many of us live in industrialized cities where the complexity of city life and materialism is rampant and we overlook the nature around us even during the holidays. However, we all have an innate tendency to appreciate nature, whether it is in the form of a windowsill or a walk in the woods.

**Stop and explore:** We can stop and explore the beautiful scenery on foot instead of surveying it through a car window. Office jobs often give us some time to recuperate on weekends and this can be an excellent opportunity to book a bed and breakfast in the countryside and walk on the footpaths with a detailed map of the area. Sometimes, it is also a good idea to take a walk on the main street without a map.

**Prioritize wellbeing:** Walking can have tremendous positive effects on our physical and mental well-being. It can give us time for self-reflection, help us regain physical strength, provide social support to those we know and refresh our spirituality by observing Allah's ﷻ creations. Walking therapy has been shown to be beneficial for symptoms of depression, anxiety and burnout. It's a way to slow down our lives and take a moment to reflect on the world around us, achieve spiritual relaxation and stay physically fit.

The Prophet ﷺ also emphasized the importance of walking. He once said, "A strong believer is better and more beloved to Allah than a weak believer, while there is good in both; Your body has a right over you" (Ibn Majah 79, Bukhari 5199).

**Interactive walks:** These days, local museums offer interactive walks in parks where native vegetation and wildflowers are labeled, along with the historical background of the area. Each numbered title on the trail map encourages stopping and learning about the plants and area's history. Riverfront trails, when available, are another great way to do a walking activity in town.

"Find and explore the forest. Take it slowly and forget about what would make a nice Instagram picture. Instead, listen to the wind in the leaves, watch the sun bounce off the branches, take a deep breath and see what smells you can detect. Try to visit the same spot several times a year, so you can appreciate how it changes over the seasons. Say hi to the first day of spring, summer, autumn and winter. Go alone or invite people to join you." – Miek Wiking, The Little Book of Lykke[6]

## Wellness Retreat

*"Give close relatives their due, as well as the poor and (needy) travellers. And do not spend wastefully. Surely, the wasteful are (like) brothers to the devils. And the Devil is ever ungrateful to his Lord."* (Qur'an 17:26-27)

Humans have long known that travel can enhance wellness. However, the concept of a wellness retreat is relatively new. With the progress of modern technology, people have found their daily lives increasingly busy and monotonous, leading to burnout and dissatisfaction. Hence, the idea of a wellness retreat emerged. It involves travelling to a place to improve one's overall health and reconnect with oneself to be more effective when returning to regular life. A wellness retreat typically includes spas, massages, saunas and superfood diets using healthy ingredients and supplements. There are wellness experts who guide participants on their eating habits and relaxation techniques. The goal is to cultivate healthier habits and leave the retreat feeling fresh and rejuvenated. However, the one drawback of wellness retreats is their cost. A single night's stay at a wellness resort in Arizona can cost up to $2000, making it an option only for the wealthy. Additionally, it is wasteful spending, as one is essentially paying for nature walks and massages that can be enjoyed outside of a resort. One can enjoy a similar experience to a highly rated retreat by designing one's own trip as a wellness trip. Some common tips recommended by experts include:

**Sleep**: It is essential to take a break from the blue light of screens and develop a regular sleeping schedule to restore wellness. To practice sleep hygiene, it is recommended to sleep around the same time every night and wake up at the same time in the morning. Also, ensure the room is dark, quiet and comfortable to ensure a restful night's sleep.

**Move**: Achieving a healthy balance in our body is crucial and one way to do that is by finding hiking trails and going for a walk every morning during the holiday. Staying active throughout the day and avoiding overactivity are also included in this.

**Read**: Unlike others who may spend time reading a fictional tale, a Muslim can utilize the same time to reconnect with the Qur'an and revive one's spiritual energy. The Qur'an is the book that talks to us if we read it the way it should be read. Scholars recommend that we should read the Qur'an as if we are the sole receiver of the message. When a verse with a command is recited, we must stop and think whether we follow the command or not. If not, we must plan to do it from now on.

> ***"And We have cited for people all sorts of examples in this Qur'an, so that they may receive the message." (Qur'an 39:27)***

**Relax**: Whether it involves going to a spa or having a tea ritual with friends and family, relaxation of our mind is essential to clear the effects of monotony and burnout.

**Sun and steam**: Sunbathing and steaming are two effective ways to relax. Sunbathing helps get vitamin D and the steam of the sauna has been shown to improve our immune system by activating disease-fighting white blood cells.

**Eat**: Eating right involves eliminating dietary toxins, foods that contain pesticides and artificial sweeteners and genetically modified foods from our diet.[5] It also means paying close attention to portion sizes, meal timing, the duration of our meals and how we digest our food. The goal is to address a common problem, "leaky gut", which can cause altered bowel habits, bloating and abdominal cramps. The condition is caused by an imbalance in fiber intake, which prevents the gut microbiome from producing enough compounds to repair the gut lining. This triggers an immune reaction that leads to inflammation.

**Superfoods**: Superfoods are an essential part of any wellness retreat. They are nutrient-rich foods that are great for our health. We must reintroduce superfoods, i.e., fiber and nutritionally rich fruits, vegetables, nuts and seeds in our diet. The list is long; however, some of the common superstar foods include sweet potatoes (high in carotenoids and fiber), mangoes (high in vitamin C), leafy greens (high fiber, vitamin A, C, K), garbanzo beans and legumes (high fiber, zinc, iron), plain yogurt (probiotic), wild salmon (high in omega-3 fats), squashes (high in carotenoids, vitamin C and fiber), watermelon (high in vitamin C and A), medicinal mushrooms, herbs and spices (high in antioxidants) and oatmeal (high in fiber). By incorporating these foods into our diet, we can improve our overall health and wellbeing.[7]

> ***"With it He causes to grow for you the crops, the olives, the date palms, the grapes and every kind of fruit. In this is indeed an evident proof and a manifest sign for people who give thought." (Qur'an 16:11)***

A good wellness retreat, whether given at a resort or arranged on our own, restores the body naturally, which is sometimes needed to restore the balance of a healthy life.[8] In modern day living, it is natural for one to feel overwhelmed with the busy routine. However, for believers, any wellness retreat is incomplete without the *dhikr* of the Almighty. Medieval Muslims rarely travelled far from home, but still managed to maintain a healthy balance in their lives. They did not feel burnout or despair from the monotony because of an achievable pace of life and a strong connection with Allah ﷻ.

## Better Mental Health

*"And whoever fears Allah and keeps his duty to Him, He will make a way for him to get out (from every difficulty) and He will provide for him from (sources) he never could imagine. And whosoever puts his trust in Allah, then He will suffice for him. Verily, Allah will accomplish His purpose. Indeed, Allah has set a measure for all things."* (Qur'an 65:2-3)

Just like physical disease, mental health issues such as anxiety and depression are also trials from Allah. Unfortunately, poor mental health carries a taboo with it and people avoid going to a psychologist despite having clinical symptoms of depression. Additionally, someone from a religious background is judged on his acts of worship if he confesses to feeling low. Having a mental breakdown should be taken seriously and the first step is acknowledging that one is suffering from it. Travel can help improve the symptoms of burnout and depression. However, a few key points may be helpful:

**Avoiding aimless travel:** When planning to travel for a spiritual retreat or to get help from depression, we must remember not to lose focus or go without planning. The purpose of travel, when done to improve mental wellbeing, is to get out of the depressed mindset of daily life. It may involve practicing mindfulness, forming a new habit or leaving a bad habit. However, having a pre-planned itinerary is crucial or the journey may cause more anxiety rather than improve it.

**Recalling the purpose:** Whether on a hike or by the beach, we must recall the purpose of our bodily existence. This world and everything in it are a temporary abode and Allah has given us a guidebook on our eternal life in detail. The sole purpose of our time in *dunya* is to recognize our Creator and serve His creations. There is more to life beyond worldly gains and losses. Recalling our purpose helps preserve our cognitive functioning and lower the rate of depression.

*And seek the (betterment of) the Ultimate Abode with what Allah has given to you and do not neglect your share from this world and do good as Allah did good to you and do not seek to make mischief in the land. Surely, Allah does not like the mischief-makers." (Qur'an 28:77)*

**Focusing on the present:** Our brains are pliable and adapt to changing circumstances. A new habit can be formed at any time. All it takes is practice and concentration to restore our attention to the present and not worry about what happens in the future. Taking social media breaks may help us with it. Consequently, we become more aware of the time we spend.

**Practicing gratitude:** Whether a verbal recall of what we are grateful for or writing it in a journal, practicing gratitude is a cornerstone in achieving mental wellbeing. It brings self-acceptance, attracts positive relationships and enhances spirituality. Gratitude draws our focus on what we have, such as the eyes that see, ears that hear, a tongue that talks and so on. As long as we are alive, we always have time to make *du'ā'* and change our life through supplications.

> *"...(only) a few of My servants are (truly) grateful." (Qur'an 34:13)*

**Avoid complaining:** Negative emotions during travel are detrimental to someone with depression. Complaining, which is the opposite of gratitude, is one such emotion. It brings many negative elements with it, like a domino effect and makes one a victim of circumstances. Thus, deep self-reflection is needed. As Muslims, we can take any unwanted circumstance as the decree of Allah and expect a better outcome from it by trusting His plan. In a hadith, the Prophet ﷺ said, "Strive for which will benefit you, seek help from Allah ﷾, do not be weak and do not say, 'If I had done such and such, the situation would be such and such,' but say, 'Allah has decreed and what He wishes, He does'" (Ibn Majah 79).

**Avoiding competition:** Unfortunately, travelling is often seen as a sign of luxury and ease. Travelling, in fact, is not a measure of success but rather a type of test. A traveller who journeys through the world but skips prayers, misses the recitation of the Qur'an and also forgoes other commands of Allah ﷻ destroys his account of deeds. While poverty and wealth are both tests, wealth is a bigger test as it is easy to forget about *Ākhirah* when one lives surrounded by blessings.

*"(He is the One) Who created death and life in order to test which of you is best in deeds. And He is the Almighty, All-Forgiving."* (Qur'an 67:2)

As Muslims, we must remember that a moderate livelihood with *taqwā* is better than extravagance with *ghaflah*. Fame, wealth and impressive social circles are not the parameters of success but rather a source of jealousy and unhealthy comparison. Those who travel more than us must be a source of inspiration, not misery.

*"Competition for more (gains) diverts you (from Allah)."* (Qur'an 102:1)

*"Or is it that they are jealous of people over what Allah has given them of His bounty, while We have given to the House of Ibrahim the Book and the wisdom and We have given to them a great kingdom?"* (Qur'an 4:54)

Sometimes hardships land on us like freezing rain, yet we must stay firm as mountains. Once the trial is over, there is a reward that awaits for the one who remained patient. Patience comes only through Allah ﷻ and those who believe in Allah ﷻ face difficulties with firm resolution. Travelling through the land, observing the open book of creation and appreciating the many wonders are good for us. It broadens our mind and replaces depression with delight.

## Jetlag

*"And we made sleep a thing for rest."* (Qur'an 78:9)

Travelling long distances across several time zones is known to cause a disruption in the connection between the time on the clock and our body's internal biological clock, called the circadian rhythm. This may result in a discordant physical, mental and behavioural condition that may last for up to 24 hours or more, commonly referred to as jetlag. Our sleep-wake cycle is heavily influenced by the natural rhythms of daylight and darkness.[9] As a result, bodily functions such as blood pressure, hunger and satiety, digestion and the release of sleep/wake hormones are balanced. Jetlag occurs when these rhythms are disrupted due to a longer flight. Symptoms of jetlag may include daytime fatigue, poor focus, stomach upset such as constipation or diarrhea, mood changes and a general feeling of being unwell. These symptoms usually surface within a day or two after arriving at the destination.

Jetlag typically occurs when an air traveller crosses at least two time zones. However, not everyone experiences jetlag. There are certain risk factors that can make us more prone to it, such as poor fitness with no regular exercise or walking habits, older age or pre-departure stress. Interestingly, flying westward and flying overnight also increases the risk of getting jetlag. To combat the symptoms of jetlag, try the following:

**More melatonin**: Jetlag occurs when melatonin production, which requires sun exposure, is reduced in our body. Melatonin is a sleep hormone which is released by our brain when exposed to darkness and it controls our sleep-wake cycles.[10] When jetlag is expected, such as in an overnight flight, one may take over-the-counter melatonin tablets to help with sleep. The usual recommended dose is between 1-3 mg during the flight and for a night or two at the travel destination (although consultation with your doctor is recommended).

**Daytime flight**: Choosing a daytime flight can be a strategic move in combating jetlag. Sunlight plays a key role in influencing our circadian rhythm. Arriving at the destination while the sun is still out gives the body time to adjust to the new sleep times. It's also beneficial to get sun exposure at the airport by sitting closer to the windows before boarding.

**More movement**: Take regular walking breaks during a long flight, especially if it's overnight. One may also set a reminder to take a quick walk every hour or two.

**Resetting the clock**: Set the time of your destination on your watch is helpful in preparing your mind to adjust to the new time zone.

**Readjust your sleep schedule**: When travelling to the east, try to go to bed an hour earlier each night to adjust to the time zone. When going towards the west, try sleeping an hour later. One can start this practice a few days before travel to avoid jetlag.

**Hydration**: This is an important aspect when experiencing jetlag, as dehydration may make the symptoms worse. Drinking plenty of fluids during and after the flight is highly recommended, especially during long-distance travel.

**Foot massage**: A foot massage can promote good sleep and is recommended by experts when one suffers from insomnia or poor sleep patterns.

**Online help**: Jet Lag Rooster is an online application that creates a customized plan to combat jetlag based on flight length, the length of daylight and the number of time zones crossed. It also provides a step-by-step guide with recommendations on sleep timing, melatonin intake and other ideas to adjust to the new time zone.

**Avoid sleeping pills**: It is not recommended to take sleeping pills other than melatonin to fight jetlag. Taking sleep aids disrupts our natural sleep habits and can make us dependent on them.

> ***"It is Allah Who receives the souls at the time of death and those that do not die during their sleep. He keeps those (souls) for which He has ordained death and sends the rest (back to their bodies) for a term appointed..." (Qur'an 39:42)***

- Eat balanced nutrients.
- Avoid chain restaurants.
- Try different varieties of food.
- Eat more earlier in the day and less at night.
- Visit the local grocery store at your destination.
- Plan ahead, researching restaurants before you leave.
- Hydration is important: don't forget your water bottle.
- It is okay to cheat, but eat healthier in the following meal.
- Remember that travel is for rest and recharge.

# Travelling as a Muslim Family

Vacationing with children can be an excellent way to strengthen family bonds. Travelling provides an opportunity for children to learn about the world, broaden their horizons and develop empathy. It also offers a chance to impart Islamic teachings while exploring the wonders of Allah's creation. When families travel together, they create lasting memories and spend quality time with each other. In this section, we will explore how Muslim families can maximize their holiday time while also earning rewards and gaining knowledge.

Family travel can be challenging, especially when children are young, yet it can become one of the most enriching experiences in life. Our Prophet ﷺ used to travel with his family, usually his wives, when embarking on a journey (Ibn Majah 2347). Oftentimes, parents assume that travelling with children is pointless because they might not remember the trip. However, it is important to note that young minds retain subconscious memories that help them better understand new circumstances in the future. All it needs is good planning, careful consideration of travel destinations and keeping in mind that the experience we give to our children through travel makes all the hard work worthwhile.

One of the most crucial aspects of family travel is finding a balance that caters to the needs of everyone involved. It's highly recommended to include children in the planning process, allowing them to share their preferences and ideas, such as places they would like to visit and activities they would like to do during the trip. Older kids can also participate in selecting their desired locations, packing their bags and choosing what they would like to take with them.

Although family trips may seem more expensive than travelling solo or with a spouse, a well-planned itinerary can help manage the expenses. Parents should plan the trip not just for leisure or shopping purposes but for the overall experience and education it offers. Visiting a place with limited financial resources can teach children more than any high-end marketplace. Moreover, experiences that enrich their minds about the remembrance of Allah ﷻ and the knowledge of His creations are worth much more than any material possession in this world.

It is important to remember that children are our most valuable assets for the *Ākhirah*. The better their upbringing, the more rewards parents can receive.

## Digital Detox

Going on a trip does not mean children must avoid their tablets and cell phones altogether, as they may need them during air travel or on road trips. However, it is essential to have a plan for a digital detox to help them break their screen addiction. Vacations must never be about spending all our time on screens and cameras. Here are a few quick tips that might be helpful for this purpose.

1. Retreat time: It is important to set expectations before the trip. Parents need to explain to their children that travelling together is an opportunity to bond, appreciate nature and relax. Not everything needs to be shared on social media.

2. Trust their memory: Nowadays, children think that anything that is not recorded will be forgotten. It is important to teach them to trust their memory

rather than relying on the camera. Sometimes, parents are too busy taking videos and photos of their children instead of enjoying the moment with them, like observing a waterfall.

3. Four-photos rule: Parents can limit the number of photos taken on a family trip. A good rule of thumb is to take four to five photos a day. This can help children avoid unrestrained camera use and learn to be more present.

4. Experience: Parents should teach their children that it's about experiencing a place, not just visiting it or taking photos. When visiting historical sites, for example, imagine what it was like to live there.

5. Careful selection of destinations: Choose a destination that introduces children to a new world, away from screens. Whether it is a mountain hike or a kayaking tour, young children immerse themselves in the moment and forget about their tablets and monitors.

## Learning Holidays

*Did you not realize that purity of Allah is proclaimed by all those in the heavens and the earth and by the birds with their wings spread out? Everyone knows one's own (way of) praying (to Allah) and one's own (way of) proclaiming Allah's purity. And Allah knows well what they do.* (Qur'an 24:41)

A successful vacation with children is one that broadens their horizons in the classroom. A learning holiday not only enhances their knowledge but also grows their interest in observing the details of their environment. An interesting way to have an enlightening trip is to capitalize on journeys that link to what they learn at school. The following are a few ways a learning holiday can be turned into a wholesome family excursion.

**Books and reading:** Taking kids to the bookstore or the library and getting books on what they might see on the upcoming trip is a great way to prepare them – for example, reading about birds when visiting a nature reserve or acquainting themselves with dinosaurs if a dinosaur museum is on the itinerary. Similarly, books on geology are helpful when visiting a place like Alaska, where most of the land is permafrost. Such a vacation will increase their interest in the trip and help them retain knowledge.

**Storytelling:** Engaging children in learning while on holiday can be achieved through different methods. One fantastic way is through storytelling. Parents can enlighten their children with the stories of the Prophets. For example, when visiting a hilly area, parents can tell their children about Prophet Musa عليه السلام and his climb up Mount Toor. Similarly, when going whale-watching, parents can narrate the story of Prophet Yunus عليه السلام and if visiting a camel farm, parents can discuss the story of Prophet Saleh عليه السلام.

**Firsthand experience:** Another way to make learning enjoyable for children is by giving them firsthand experiences. Staying on a farm (agritourism) or visiting a petting zoo can be a great hands-on experience for children. They learn about nature and farming while spending time feeding the animals. Drive-through safaris can also be an incredible experience for children to see animals in their natural habitat. While feeding the animals through the car window, parents can teach their children about the rewards of feeding the hungry, even if it is an animal.

**Pictures and footprints:** During a learning holiday, children can be taught to appreciate and respect nature by taking pictures and leaving nothing but footprints. Parents can also educate them about the importance of not feeding wild animals and following wildlife regulations.

**Local handicrafts:** Additionally, children enjoy skill development activities such as learning local handicrafts. They can learn age-appropriate handicrafts like basket-weaving, wildflower-picking, ceramic-making, flower-pressing and more.

**Educational museums:** An educational vacation with children can be both fun and enriching. Even lesser-known museums, such as those dedicated to rural life, mining, archeology or taxidermy, can be exciting for kids. Science exhibitions and observatories are also great options. In fact, any small yet authentic museum is better than a modern one with a virtual display of collections.

**Backyard camping:** Sometimes we look for such far-out vacation destinations when really children can enjoy just as much from exploring their neighbourhood. At times, it may not be possible to travel during the holidays and that is when parents can make a creative plan for a learning holiday while staying at home. For instance, children can explore the botanical details of trees and shrubs in their local park or set up a tent in their backyard for a story session around a small bonfire. Parents can also involve their kids in planning an exploration of their city to learn more about the area.

A learning holiday broadens children's horizons. In the long run, anything learned with enjoyment can leave a lasting impact on their minds, which sometimes can help them decide their future careers.

## Explore Nature with Children

We are living in a time when both parents and children are hyperconnected to the screens. The compulsive use of the internet has made us oblivious to the natural world around us and we encounter only a fraction of the population travelling outdoors or taking their children with them. This is particularly true in Muslim societies. As a result, most of us are unfamiliar with the names of the wildflowers growing near our homes or the birds in our gardens. Allah has created nature and all living beings for the benefit of humans. He has kept intricate details in it for us to observe and learn. A whole new world opens when we enlighten ourselves with the knowledge of the natural world.

*"Do you not see that Allah causes the night to merge into the day and the day into the night and has subjected the sun and the moon, each orbiting for an appointed term and that Allah is All-Aware of what you do?"* (Qur'an 31:29)

Someone wisely said that children learn by observing their parents' actions, not by what they are told to do. With adults experiencing higher rates of burnout and children facing an alarming escalation of depression and anxiety, it is crucial that parents introduce their children to the elements of nature. Vacations are the best times for nature therapy. Children thrive in fresh air and they enjoy an outdoor adventure during holidays. While schools now offer summer camps in the mountainous wilderness, the best trips are where parents actively experience nature with their children. The goal is to connect children with the natural world in a way that reminds them of Allah's magnificence and the stories of His prophets.

**Nature walks:** Children have a different relation to nature walks than adults. They find nature mysterious and enchanting as they observe the changes that occur from season to season, from the wildflowers in the spring to the falling leaves of autumn. They like noticing the details. We can sharpen their observation by asking them to notice the trees and learn their names, find a flock of geese and get to know their local fauna. It is also valuable for children to learn about soil, as that helps them understand the importance of clean soil and how it affects the quality of our food. We can start with small strolls and bring their focus to the details of nature as they walk, noticing for example the shapes of leaves, the petals of flowers, the wild grass on the sidewalks and the smell of pine trees and so on. We can also teach them to remember Allah and reflect on His creations as we walk. Children can be reminded of the trees of *Jannah* (Paradise) as they explore trees in this world. The

Prophet ﷺ said, "In Paradise, there is a tree under the shadow of which a rider can travel for a hundred years" (Muslim 2826a).

**Know the names:** If we know something by its name, there are chances that we have more knowledge about it. When it comes to nature, having an expanded vocabulary is useful. Children who carefully observe nature can appreciate that everything they see reflects the diversity of our planet. Furthermore, learning the names of trees and flowers while exploring nature creates a lasting memory.

**Nature as a metaphor:** Children can also learn educational insights as they go by using nature as a metaphor. For example, honeybees land on flowers but do not damage them; rather, they are compassionate and respectful. Additionally, they teach us about hard work and dedication. Engaging stories that connect children to the natural world can be an effective way to teach valuable lessons. One such example is the verse from the Qur'an that talks about camels and how they were distinctively created: *"Do they not ever reflect on camels – how they were (masterfully) created"* (Qur'an 88:17).

*"And your Lord inspires the bees, 'Make (your) homes in the mountains, the trees and in what people construct and feed from (the flower of) any fruit (you please) and follow the ways your*

*Lord has made easy for you.' From their bellies comes forth liquid of varying colours, in which there is healing for people. Surely, in this is a sign for those who reflect."* (Qur'an 16:68-69)

**Give them tools:** Children can benefit greatly from being equipped with tools during nature walks as part of their extracurricular activities. This could include reading maps while hiking or having a list of things to look out for during the walk. Children are particularly thrilled by tools such as magnifying glasses for inspecting insects, binoculars for bird watching, pocket cameras and sketch pads.

**Junior ranger programs:** Parents can also enroll their children in junior ranger programs, which are activity-based outdoor programs affiliated with national parks and local museums. Children can document their experiences in a nature journal as they explore and learn about environmental conservation and minimizing human impact. The program also covers topics such as archeology, astronomy and cave systems; and conducts scavenger hunts and kayak tours.

As parents, it is natural for us to gravitate towards our comfort zones, especially during holidays. However, it is our responsibility to introduce them to the diverse relationships that exist among different creatures on earth. By exploring nature, we can remind them of Allah's سبحانه وتعالى

abundant blessings upon us and train them to observe His creations in the way mentioned in the Qur'an. In doing so, we are also reminding them about Jannah and directing their focus towards our ultimate destination in *Ākhirah*.

*"And to Allah belongs the dominion of the Heavens and the Earth and Allah is over all things. Indeed, in the creations of the heavens and earth and the alternation of the night and day are signs for those of understanding."* (Qur'an 3:189-190)

## A Holiday with the Qur'an

*"A Book we have sent down to you so that you may bring forth mankind from the darkness into the light."* (Qur'an 14:1)

Summer breaks are a crucial time for children. After months of tedious routine, summer holidays provide an opportunity for self-care. During this time, children may stay at their grandparents' house, go on camping trips or visit new locations with their family. Parents often plan months in advance, taking into consideration their financial status and children's wishes when deciding the holiday schedule. However, what often goes unnoticed is the amount of time children spend with the Qur'an and their relationship with it.

Parents have a responsibility to develop a bond between

their children and the Qur'an. The Qur'an is the guidebook for our temporary life in this world. It builds our relationship with Allah ﷻ and is a source of contentment from emotional and mental distress. It is our source of ultimate success in *Ākhirah* as it contains the answers to the questions we shall be asked in the grave. Therefore, developing a habit of reading the Qur'an from an early age is indispensable. Children who are raised with an interest in the Qur'an receive its *barakah* (blessing) from an early age. They are more likely to follow its commands, which changes their personality, strengthens their faith and makes them steadfast on their *deen*. Vacations are an ideal time to develop our connection with the Qur'an. As parents, we can allocate time for reading the Qur'an, understanding its meaning and discussing the take-away lessons from it. Both parents and children can avail themselves of this opportunity, as they usually stay busy in mundane routines.

"Read the Qur'an, for it will come on the Day of Resurrection and intercede for its companions." (Muslim 804)

Vacations are also a great time to change the environment of our homes and incorporate new Islamic habits. For example, we can allocate a specific time for reading the Qur'an and encourage our children to live according to its guidance. By explaining the stories of the Prophets in an interesting manner, children develop a passion for reading more about the Qur'an and learning about real heroes. The Qur'an teaches them about *sabr* (perseverance), *shukr* (gratitude), *tawbah* (repentance) and *tawakkul* (reliance) and inculcates these qualities in their personality.

*"(This is) a blessed Book which We have revealed to you, (O Prophet), so that might reflect upon its verses and people of reason may be mindful."* (Qur'an 38:29)

It is up to parents to explain the Qur'an to their children. They may choose to raise them in a secular way or follow the examples of the companions of the Prophet ﷺ, who instilled a strong bond with the Qur'an from early on. Through visualization of the scenes of *Jahannam* and the blessings of *Jannah* mentioned in the Qur'an, children can comprehend the concept of their investment in *Ākhirah*.

## Travelling with Parents

*"Your Lord has decreed that you worship none but Him and do good to parents. If any one of them or both of them reach old age, do not say to the 'uff' [a word or expression of anger or contempt] and do not scold them and address them with respectful words."* (Qur'an 17:23)

Older age comes with multiple challenges of chronic diseases and physical limitations. It may become increasingly difficult to maintain meaningful connections as social circles shrink and loved ones pass away. Consequently, elderly parents or grandparents often confine themselves to their homes. They need extra attention when they are older as they may feel reserved due to mobility issues and health problems. That is why Allah has emphasized treating parents well, because they spend their time of youth raising children. Allah ﷾ has mentioned the rights of parents in the Qur'an right after His rights to signify their status. Taking parents on a trip can be an incredibly rewarding experience, allowing multiple generations of the family to bond and create cherished memories. Furthermore, travelling has been shown to provide various health benefits for older adults, including increased physical activity that improves endurance and muscle health, as well as reduced inflammation and boosted immunity through moderate exercise such as walking.

**Expectations:** Planning a comfortable trip with older parents requires frequent communication. Having an open conversation about their expectations, preferences and concerns is important. Our parents may have a specific idea about their travel plans, such as visiting historical places and museums or focusing on nature walks. They may prefer a cruise, train journey or guided city tour. Alternatively, they may only want to spend time with their grandchildren without any preferences. In any case, it is crucial to have a conversation with everyone involved in the trip to define their expectations beforehand. Sometimes, it may be reasonable to book a tour with a tour company and let someone else handle the logistics, especially on a multi-generational trip.

**Health risks:** When planning a trip with parents, one must keep their physical fitness and energy levels into account. Depending on their health status and the nature of the journey, they may have different limitations and medical needs. Therefore, it is helpful to plan ahead by looking for restaurants that accommodate their dietary restrictions. One may also consider getting travel insurance and consulting with their primary healthcare provider, especially if they have a medical device such as a pacemaker.

**Accommodating itinerary:** When planning an itinerary for parents, it is important to look for activities that are not strenuous. Physically challenging trips may exhaust them and even increase their health risks. Instead, one may opt for more leisurely outings such as a light cruise, sightseeing tour or whale-watching. For a hiking trip, a short warm-up is helpful in preventing injury, building endurance and maintaining a healthy heart rate. Additionally, when planning a road trip, it is important to ask about the frequency of stops to ensure everyone stays comfortable.

**Back-up plans and afternoon splits:** Travelling with family can become a roller coaster ride at any time, which is why it is necessary to have a plan for unexpected situations. An organized plan with information on how to get the rental vehicle, arrival time and check-in is imperative when planning the itinerary. Be prepared with Plan B and C locations in case of sickness or inclement weather. When travelling with elderly family members, it's helpful to plan afternoon breaks so they can rest and recharge before continuing with activities. A flexible itinerary with multiple back-up plans can make the trip less stressful and more enjoyable for everyone involved.

> ***"And lower to them the wing of humility out of mercy and say, 'My Lord, have mercy upon them as they brought me up (when I was) small.' (Qur'an 17:24)***

- Utilize online resources such as AAA in the United States and AA in the United Kingdom before going on a long-distance road trip with children.
- Other helpful resources include flyingbaby.com and seatguru.com for tips on flying with babies.
- Keep them engaged by giving them a goal for the day.
- Take them on shorter hikes, letting them get used to nature walks to avoid stress in the future.
- Download a podcast on Islamic history for vacations.
- Teach them to be kind to wildlife and maintain a comfortable distance.
- Children are prone to dehydration. Avoid too many sugary drinks and keep a water bottle with them always.
- We are role models to our children; show them how to experience new things in life, such as new cuisines or new people.
- A holiday with the Qur'an is always an excellent idea.

# Travelling Responsibly

In recent times, there has been an increase in over-tourism, resulting in once-secluded wilderness areas becoming crowded tourist spots. More people than ever are visiting scenic destinations and exploring international cultures. While tourism empowers global communities by creating jobs, it can also have a detrimental effect on our ecosystem. To maintain a balance between our curiosity and consciousness, we must adopt the practice of responsible travelling. This means exploring the world while being thoughtful about the potential impact of our travel on the planet. The way we visit communities and use their resources during our travels can leave a lasting impression on the places we explore.

## A Responsible Travel Photographer

Photography has become an integral part of travelling nowadays. People take photos to capture memories of their trips. However, it is important to be responsible and mindful, ensuring that others are not unintentionally photographed without their consent. Responsible photography involves taking other people's photos or including them in our images only with their permission. Often, we see people taking photos indiscriminately without considering who might be in the background. The same goes for videography. Young travellers who create vlogs often include everyone in their filming without thinking twice. Unfortunately, this trend is becoming common even in Muslim societies, where people film strangers' worship and post it on social media. Whether it is a mosque or a marketplace, pictures are being taken recklessly without asking for permission.

Taking someone's photo or video without their consent is like stealing their possession. Just as we would not want our possessions taken without permission, we should extend the same courtesy to others. It is also important to wait for the background crowd to fade away or ask people if they are comfortable being in a snapshot or a video. As Muslims, it is a part of our faith that the angels take note of each time we infringe upon someone's rights, even if it's just the right to be asked for permission before being included in a vlog or photo. Allah ﷻ has mentioned in the Qur'an that we will be shocked to see every small sin listed in our book of deeds. This is because some things that we may consider trivial may carry a heavy burden of sins.

*"And the book (of deeds) will be placed (before them), then you will see the guilty people scared of its contents and saying, 'Woe to us! What a book is this! It has missed nothing, minor or major, but has taken it into account.' Thus, they will find whatever they did present before them and your Lord will not wrong anyone."* (Qur'an 18:49)

While Islamic scholars do not recommend visiting the worship areas of other religions, especially when one visits to endorse the place or the rituals of worship, one may still encounter a sanctified place outside the houses of worship, such as a designated site holy to the Polynesian people or a shrine belonging to a Native American tribe. The locals in these areas might be sensitive to photography or videography of their sacred landmarks. Therefore, it is best to get permission or look for photography guidelines on the website. Unfortunately, social media has made us accustomed to posting about every place we visit. People tend to make vlogs without asking permission. This can inadvertently leave a negative impression of Muslims in these communities. While we follow the rules of our mosques, we must also respect areas that belong to other communities.

## Conscious Online Sharing

*"And do not turn your cheek away from people and do not walk on the earth haughtily. Surely, Allah does not like anyone who is arrogant, proud..."* (Qur'an 31:18)

The digital presence of a traveller is not limited to using social media, photography or vlogging, but also includes what is shared along the way. Responsible online sharing has many aspects, such as online reviews, geotagging, tagging others who travel with us, creating hashtags and promoting them and so on. However, it is easy to fall into the trap of oversharing and revealing too many details about our personal life and travel plans. Therefore, it is important to be mindful of our online presence, especially when we travel.

**Avoid geotagging:** One of the ways to maintain a responsible online presence is to avoid geotagging. Geotagging means sharing our online location as we travel. While it may be acceptable to update family and friends via social media, not everyone needs to know our whereabouts. Geotagging is often done by amateur tourists who may want to gain more followers by becoming a part of more hashtags. However, experienced travellers and campers strictly avoid such flamboyance. Geotagging may also involve sharing upcoming travel plans unnecessarily. Such acts only make us more vulnerable to cyberbullying and theft and increase our chances of attracting unwanted attention.

**Tagging without permission:** Tagging others without their permission is unfortunately a common issue on social media. People tag others in photos and videos without consent, which compromises everyone's privacy and security. When it comes to being a good traveller, one's character is judged by how they treat their fellow travellers. This includes respecting their time, helping them with their needs and showing them sympathy. Additionally, a good travel companion should help us in our actions and on our spiritual journey. They should remind us and guide us when we forget. As the Prophet ﷺ said, "Every man follows the religion of his friend."

**Online reviews:** Online reviews are a common way for people to share their experiences with restaurants, hotels and other businesses. However, it is important to be mindful of what we write. While serious issues like mixing halal meat with haram or the presence of alcohol in sauces should be reported, the most negative reviews are about things like delayed service, bland food or an unappealing atmosphere. It is not fair to rebuke a restaurant or hotel because the food was not warm enough or a box of tissues was missing in the hotel room. Instead of writing negative reviews, it is more thoughtful to provide direct feedback to the working staff. A constructive critique can help them improve their services. We should also remember that our negative comments can have a real impact on the people who work at these businesses, especially those who earn low wages. As responsible travellers we have the example of our beloved Prophet ﷺ who always preferred forgiveness and understanding.

Abu Hurairah narrated, "The Prophet ﷺ never criticized any food, but he used to eat it if he liked the food and leave it if he disliked it" (Bukhari 5409).

**Comparing landscapes:** Comparing nature areas is a common habit among young travellers who are new to exploring national parks and forest conservations. They tend to post excessively about a place and invite crowds, while also comparing every detail of one park with another. For instance, amateur hikers may comment on the colour or shape of a mountain in South Dakota and compare it with the one in Hawai'i. Similarly, tourists may use harsh words for the trees in certain areas and mock the river or a lake in another. However, a Muslim traveller who appreciates nature and explores the world with *taqwā* rarely does that, because whether it is a mountain range in Uzbekistan or an island in Indonesia, the Creator is the same. Thus, humility comes in when Allah's created world is observed keeping Him and His creativity in mind. Nature is created with perfection, with an absolute harmony between its geological details and atmospheric conditions.

*"He Who created all things in the best way and He began the creation of man from clay..."* (Qur'an 32:7)

These are some examples of the changing landscape in travelling and how modern technology is affecting it. We need to decide how to take advantage of the opportunities given to us, by always keeping the consciousness of Allah with us.

## Supporting the Local Economy

"Allah is Kind and loves kindness and He rewards for kindness in a way that He does not reward for harshness." (Ahmad 902)

According to the United Nations Tourism Organization, only about five percent of a traveller's expenditure is utilized for the benefit of the local community. The remaining amount is spent on well-known brands. It is a common misconception that off-beat destinations and unknown lodges are unsafe when compared to chain hotels. While this may be true in a few cases, most of the time, locally-owned guesthouses and small lodges are the best places to meet helpful and open-hearted people. They can provide excellent directions to various locations, reveal some secret local discounts and go out of their way to help guests in case of emergencies.

We are often surprised by the hospitality and courtesy of locals. Small motels and homestays offer some of the most memorable experiences to travellers. This is because the people who run these local lodges are deeply rooted in their communities and have the most interesting stories about the history of the area. As a responsible traveller, there are several ways one can help the locals in the area.

- **Local first:** When travelling, it's always best to support local businesses as much as possible. Look for a family-owned lodge or guesthouse to get a more authentic experience of the place we are visiting. Ask the owners about access to local communities, as this can enhance our experience even further. By staying at a locally owned business, we indirectly support local employees, food-providers and other related small businesses. It's also an opportunity to leave a positive impression as a Muslim, especially when exploring a non-Muslim country.

- **Bed and breakfast**: Staying in a bed and breakfast or Airbnb is another good option. However, make sure to avoid staying with a non-mahram and that there are no dogs in the house. As Muslims, we do not hold anything against animals, but it is important to note that the presence of a dog inside the house limits the entrance of angels of mercy upon us, as mentioned in a hadith of the Prophet ﷺ.
- **Branded hotels:** When choosing a chain hotel for lodging, it is also important to inquire about their environmental policies. We can ask the front desk if they follow eco-friendly guidelines and how they can make our experience more environmentally friendly. A hotel that is truly eco-friendly will usually provide a note in the room requesting mindful water use, towel reuse and energy consumption. On a side note, local bed and breakfasts and guesthouses can be a great source of inspiration for our own homes. For instance, if the hosts are highly organized and maintain a clean environment, it can motivate us to keep our living space in pristine condition as well. Their minimalistic lifestyle can also inspire us to declutter and keep fewer things in our own homes.

## Avoiding *Israaf* (Wastage)

"Verily Allah likes three things for you and He disapproves three things for you. He is pleased with you that you worship Him and associate nor anything with Him, that you hold fast the rope of Allah and be not scattered; and He disapproves for you irrelevant talk, persistent questioning and wasting of wealth." (Muslim 1715)

As travellers, especially those with children, it's easy to fall into a habit of careless use of hotel amenities, such as towels, toiletries and utilities. This can amount to unnecessary waste and a disregard for the resources at our disposal. It's crucial to remember that we are accountable for our actions, even when on vacation. Therefore, we must strive to practice responsible living during our travels, making conscious decisions about our use of resources, even those provided for free.

### *".... and do not be extravagant." (Qur'an 7:31)*

*Israaf* does not only apply to the money. It also includes the use of everyday items, such as light, water and electricity. The concept of responsible living was introduced by our beloved Prophet ﷺ, who strictly forbade wastage even when performing ablution with river water. For his *wudu*, he only used about 600 ml of water (Bukhari 201). In another hadith, he emphasized that we will be held accountable for the resources we have been given and how we use them (Tirmidhi 3358). We must avoid being wasteful even when travelling. Let's explore some ways we can adopt responsible living during travel to improve ourselves.

1. Turn off lights and air conditioning. Even though we do not pay the hotel's electricity bill, it is still our responsibility to turn off the lights and air conditioning to avoid wasting resources.

2. Bring our own water bottle. It is not only healthy but also reduces plastic use. Additionally, most hotels have a refilling water station in their gym and the staff usually allow its use.

3. Bring our own toiletries. Our bodies are more habituated to the brands we use at home anyway. Therefore, it is best to bring personal toiletries in travel-size containers. Moreover, the quality of our personal toiletries is much superior to the free items provided by the hotels.

4. Avoid wasting towels. Instead, reuse the given set of towels according to your needs.

5. Avoid taking a pen and notepad from the hotel

room. It is for our use in the hotel room. We may use it if there is an urgent need to take notes. However, the housekeeping staff usually expect us to leave the pen and leftover notepad in the room.

"*...and those who, when they spend, are neither extravagant nor miserly and it (i.e. their spending) is moderate in between (the two extremes).*" (Qur'an 25:67)

## Practice Minimalism

"Be in this world as if you were a stranger or a traveller along a path." (Bukhari 6416)

There is a growing trend among young travellers, primarily from Europe, to travel minimally. It involves booking accommodation in small cabins in forests or renting tiny houses. The size of these accommodations is typically between 300 and 500 square feet. The idea of minimalistic travel was first introduced in the West by naturalist and poet Henry David Thoreau, who built a small cabin in the woods for peaceful living.

Today, businesses like Airbnb promote cabin rentals and some people now prefer staying in tiny houses for various reasons. The small space naturally cuts down on distractions and slows down the pace of life. Families get to enjoy quality time together away from the noise of the city. The proximity to nature allows for early morning hikes, peaceful soundscapes and a break from busy traffic. Additionally, this trend helps in environmental conservation as most tiny houses are built using sustainable materials. They often have solar panels, propane heaters and a self-sustaining water supply. Nowadays, people also book tiny houses for holidays to experience small-living and opt for cabin living due to the high market prices of housing and real estate collapses.

Vacationing in a tiny house is a perfect way to experience a simpler way of living, with only the necessary possessions. This idea is especially meaningful for Muslims, as our Prophet ﷺ has shown us how to live with less while still enjoying life with family and friends. His eco-friendly and responsible lifestyle was an example of living like a traveller, avoiding isolation and extravagance. As Muslims, we can consider booking a tiny house for a vacation at least once to understand that happiness does not depend on material possessions. It can also help us imagine a life where we can live minimally in a world of consumerism and excess.

Small-space living, even if it's just for a few days, can offer many benefits. It provides us with more time to take nature walks, perform prayers without any distractions and recite more Qur'an. By living in a smaller space, we learn to direct our focus on the small pleasures in life, which are the real essence of our lives. It helps us to eliminate the greed of always wanting more. In essence, we learn to live with less, which is something that our Prophet ﷺ demonstrated in his everyday life.

> ***"Know well that the worldly life is but a play and an amusement and a show of beauty and exchange of boastful claims between you..." (Qur'an 57:20)***

# Budget Friendly Travel

Travelling is often associated with going over budget. The temptation to purchase new things can be strong, but it ultimately leads to more clutter and a compromised travel budget that can take months to recover from. However, there are plenty of ways that travellers can still have meaningful experiences while staying within their estimated budget. In this section, we will learn strategies to help travellers make their travel more meaningful without breaking the bank.

## Wallet-Friendly Itinerary

*"...those who, when they spend, are not extravagant and not niggardly, but hold a just (balance) between those extremes..."* (Qur'an 25:67)

Not everyone who travels is financially prosperous. In fact, most people belong to the modest-to-moderate income group. These middle-class travellers often follow a few standard rules to make their itinerary budget friendly.

**Travelling off-season:** Off-season travel means going to a holiday destination when crowds are minimal. It may not favour those with families, as the school-going children may not get time off from school during term. For others, off-season travel may be a favourable option. The specific months may vary depending on the geographical location and it is necessary to do some research beforehand. For instance, spring and autumn are considered off-season months in the US and other Western countries. While the weather may still be cold in early spring and late autumn, the crowds are minimal and so are the rates for airfares, hotels and cruises. Travelling during the offseason also allows for enjoying the serenity of nature's beauty and solitude on hiking trails.

**Mode of transportation:** Air tickets and rental cars are usually expensive, which is why many budget-conscious travellers prefer other modes of transportation such as a long train journey or a cruise. These options may take longer but are often worth the time and money. Additionally, many budget-friendly travellers believe that travel is about creating a contrast from everyday life, refreshing the mind and creating space for productivity. Therefore, they may also opt for a road trip in their own vehicle as it is a relatively cheaper option.

**Vacation length**: Wallet-friendly vacations are often longer in duration and fewer in number per year. Moving quickly from place to place can be costly, which is why a traveller who explores a new destination, either solo or with family, can spend more leisure time staying for longer and learn more about the place. This not only creates lasting memories but also allows for a more immersive experience.

**Relatives:** Relatives can be a great source of support when it comes to finding a place to stay. Whether it's first cousins, distant relatives, friends of our parents, old neighbours or other family ties, they can offer us a safe and comfortable place to stay. This not only helps us save money, but also strengthens our familial bonds and can sometimes lead to life-long friendships.

**Same thing, different location**: For budget-conscious travellers, it's always a good idea to find a cheaper option for an expensive experience. For example, if seeing the northern lights is on the bucket list, it might not matter whether we see them in Alaska or in northern Minnesota. The same applies to beach holidays or autumn getaways. By exploring different locations, we can still have a great experience without crossing budget limits.

**Traveller, not a tourist**: As a traveller, we should aim to immerse ourselves in the local culture rather than following the typical tourist route. A luxurious hotel and fancy restaurant do not necessarily equate to a fulfilling vacation. We can opt to stay in a more authentic and less touristy place and dine in local restaurants to experience the local cuisine. This can often lead to a more enjoyable and cost-effective trip.

**Walking more:** Walking is an excellent way to save money and create lasting memories. By walking, we can discover the area in greater detail and appreciate the intricate attributes around us, such as a beautiful topiary or a local store selling medicinal oils. We may even encounter hidden gems while walking to the nearest bus stop or exploring nearby cottages. Walking can be an exciting adventure, especially when travelling with children. It is a free and enjoyable way to explore the place we are visiting.

## Camping for Muslims

*"He created the Heavens and the earth for just purpose. He wraps the night over the day and He wraps the day over the night and He has put the sun and the moon under His command, each of them moving for an appointed term. Remember, He is the Mighty, the Most Forgiving."* (Qur'an 39:5)

Camping has been a part of human history since ancient times, with people taking breaks during long journeys to rest and camp along the way. Even during the time of our Prophet ﷺ, people went on journeys that could last weeks or months. He ﷺ advised travellers to let their camels graze when travelling through fertile lands, to hurry when crossing dry areas and to avoid setting up camp near roads as they attract wild animals and poisonous insects at night (Tirmidhi 2858).

Nowadays, camping involves spending a night in the wilderness in a tent or camper van. It typically involves sleeping outdoors, cooking meals over an open fire and enjoying the natural surroundings. For Muslims, camping requires additional considerations, such as access to water and restrooms, knowing the direction of *qibla* for prayer and ensuring the safety of the camping area for the family. Nonetheless, camping is a popular activity among Muslim youth, with schools and colleges often organizing camping trips.

**Camping tent:** Camping in the wilderness is an outdoor adventure that takes us out of our comfort zone. While everyone's reason for camping may be different, the main theme is to satisfy our curiosity by staying inside the forest with minimal resources. Most people want to connect with the basics of life again and camping provides an opportunity for them to adjust to the rhythms of nature. The surrounding nature seems more alive when we camp. We can hear the sound of rustling leaves as the wind blows through the trees and marvel at the beauty of the stars and passing clouds. There is so much to see and observe in nature. Our mundane daily habits become more mindful and we can pray with more concentration as we are not disturbed by the chores of daily life and social media. The diet gets simpler and more scheduled and we get to eat together. While camping, our days are dictated by our prayer times, meals and other physical activities; there is no rush to reach a certain destination, nor any impulse to be on social media. It is a timeless experience and a break for a good rest. Camping memories stay with us for months and years to come.

**Camper van:** Camping in a camper van is a modern version of camping where one stays in the woods inside a van equipped with toilet and kitchenette facilities. The goal is to simplify life and live away from the hustle and bustle of urban life for a few days. Some people also choose camper van living due to the high cost of residing in a city.

Camping in a camper van or in general may sound attractive, but it is not suitable for everyone. Before deciding to camp, there are some important points to consider.

- Preparation is the key: One needs to be fully prepared to stay overnight in a campground where basic life necessities are scarce. Initially, it may require an expensive shopping trip, along with getting permission for the campsite and completing the paperwork.
- Nearby camping areas: When looking for camping areas, it is always best to start from the nearest campsites, closer to home. This way, one can quickly handle any emergencies. Experts recommend choosing a campsite within an eight-hour radius from home.
- Avoid public holidays: It is advisable to avoid camping during public holidays to avoid crowds and noise pollution.

- Careful campground selection: For beginners, it is best to select a campground with basic facilities like toilets and water supply. These campgrounds are also helpful when camping with young children. Some may also offer additional amenities like tennis courts and grilling spots.

- Hiking trails: The best campsite is often the one that is near hiking trails. This keeps the experience simple and one can easily engage in physical activities like hiking to a waterfall, walking by the river or kayaking with family.

- Bring food and bedding from home: When planning for a camping trip, it is advisable for campers to bring food and bedding from home. This saves money and ensures eating healthy, home-cooked meals.

- Be prepared for the worst: It is important to be prepared for the worst, as camping trips can be unpredictable and things may not always go as planned. Although camping adventures can be exciting and push us out of our comfort zone, there may be times when we face challenges such as heavy rain, lack of sleep and cold temperatures.

An outdoor adventure in the form of camping pushes us out of our comfort zone. It can be a rewarding experience as it allows us to connect with the basic necessities of life and appreciate nature.

*"He has subjugated for you the day and the night and the sun and the moon and the stars (too) are subservient by His command. Surely, in that, there are signs for people who understand."* (Qur'an 16:12)

## Explore the Neighbourhood

"There is none amongst the Muslims who plants a tree or sows seeds and then a bird or a person or an animal eats from it, but it is regarded as a charitable gift for him." (Bukhari 2320)

In today's world, millions of people travel around the globe. With numerous countries and continents to choose from, finding a travel destination has become much easier. Every year, thousands of travel books are published, aiding in travel planning and execution. However, this trend has led to a peculiar group of travellers who explore faraway lands but are unaware of the natural beauty in their own neighbourhoods. It's not uncommon to meet someone who has travelled to Iceland to see its mountains but hasn't explored their nearby state or provincial park.

*And (He subjugated to you) whatever He created for you on the earth having varied colours. Surely, in that, there is a sign for people who accept advice.* (Qur'an 16:13)

Neighbourhood travel means exploring one's surroundings before deciding to fly off seeing exotic destinations. It is a cost-effective option that can be availed of by people of all financial backgrounds at any time of the year. Any town that we have not visited before is new to us and the excitement of exploring it can be like that of travelling to a far-off tropical island. Small towns, regardless of the country or the continent, possess hidden charms that are often overlooked by the locals. There are several ways one can indulge in neighbourhood travel and learn more about the town they live in. Not only does it save money, but it also offers the convenience of being close to home and the thrill of discovering hidden gems in our own backyard.

1. Neighbourhood travel is possible even when people have a full-time job. Weekends can be utilized for a quick getaway to the woods and exploring the area without using a map.

2. Search for museums, galleries and local stores in the locality and explore them to know what hidden treasures there in the city are you live in.

3. Look for scenic highways, country farms and low-key main streets for rural fun and simple living.

4. Sometimes, the best tour guides are a few minutes away. Look for walking tours or small boat tours in your area if you happen to have a body of water nearby.

5. Find locally sourced restaurants that serve fresh food prepared from home-grown ingredients. This can be useful when relatives or friends visit.

6. Also, find nearby archaeology sites and other historic landmarks. There are often informative tours available on these sites.

***"Have they not traveled on earth to see how was the end of those before them? They were stronger than these in power and they had tilled the land and had made it more populous than these have made it and their messengers had come to them with clear proofs. So Allah was not such as could do injustice to them, but they used to do injustice to themselves." (Qur'an 30:9)***

## Budget-Friendly Shopping

"If the son of Adam had a valley full of gold, he would like to have two valleys, for nothing fills his mouth except dust. And Allah forgives he who repents to Him." (Bukhari 6439)

One of the most remarkable things about travelling is that it can help us better understand our shopping habits. Are we prone to making impulse purchases or do we take our time to decide what we really need? Do we prefer buying well-known brands or enjoy browsing second-hand stores? Our shopping habits while travelling can also reveal great gift ideas for our loved ones. Here are some tips on how to be a conscious shopper when travelling, as Allah does not like those who waste money.

"*...and do not be extravagant. Surely, Allah does not like the extravagant.*" (Qur'an 6:141)

**Control impulse-buying**: To limit impulse buying, it's important to take a step back and distance oneself from the product for some time. Whether it means leaving the store and exploring other shops or simply walking to a different section of the same store, this will help you determine whether you really want to buy the item in question. Often, we do not realize how quickly we can adapt to being without something and start looking for the next item to buy.

"Have nothing in your house that you do not know to be useful or believe to be beautiful." – William Morris

**Want versus need:** It's important to remember the principle of "want versus need" when buying things. Sometimes, we forget to ask ourselves whether we're buying something out of necessity or if it's just to update something we already own. It is also important to consider whether the purchase is solely for social media purposes, as some people are now buying items to show them off on social media.

**Do not follow the crowd**: It is important to avoid following the crowd when it comes to making purchases. There are often people who buy T-shirts with the name of a nature area they've explored or a museum they've visited, even if they already have a dozen t-shirts at home. Such behaviour is often driven by peer pressure and the desire to keep up with others rather than any real need.

**Skip the brands:** Avoid branded clothing. It is not pleasant to see people flaunting huge logos and promoting brands for free. It is considered ostentatious and showy when one tries to indicate that they can afford a particular brand. Sometimes, low self-esteem may be the reason why people feel the need to carry a certain brand logo to fit in. These principles of ostentation go against Islamic principles of integrity and simplicity. A Muslim does not need to rely on a particular brand to show their worth, nor does a Muslim woman need to carry a specific branded bag to convey her status in society.

**Mindful Gifts:** Thoughtful gifts are loved by everyone. Despite the modern-day consumerist culture, some things still hold great value. This includes locally made products such as seasonings, spices, soaps, flavoured oils, religious gifts and locally made souvenirs. Many travellers opt to gift experiences by purchasing tickets to the parks they have just visited for their friends and family.

*"Give gifts and you will love one another."* (Adab al-Mufrad 594)

Purchasing necessary items using halal income, within one's financial means, is permissible in Islam. However, our focus tends to be on what we lack rather than realizing the sufficiency of what we already possess. Our holidays need not revolve around materialism or excessive spending. Financially responsible Muslim travellers spend in a manner that pleases Allah, avoiding credit card rewards and interest-based offers. They understand that memories are more valuable than possessions and when created with Allah's ﷻ *taqwā* in mind, they reap eternal rewards.

***"If you count the bounties of Allah, you cannot count them all. Surely, Allah is Most-Forgiving, Very-Merciful." (Qur'an 16:18)***

# Mindful Travel

Mindfulness is being aware of the present moment without judging an experience. Its purpose is to enhance calmness and relaxation in our everyday life experiences by giving deeper meaning to otherwise seemingly superficial tasks. Mindful living reduces anxiety and promotes compassion for others and the planet. In the following pages, we will explore the different aspects of mindful travelling and how they can help us feel cognizant during our trips.

## An Antidote to Burnout

*"Surely in this there is a reminder for one who has a (mindful) heart or lends an ear as a witness."* (Qur'an 50:37)

In today's modern world, multitasking has become the norm. Our lives are busy and it often feels like there needs to be more time in the day to get everything done. More people travel longer distances for work. While technology has made our lives easier, it has also introduced burnout, a condition our ancestors were unfamiliar with. Burnout is the feeling of being completely worn out from work and other responsibilities, resulting from the exhaustion of being overworked. It can lead to a lack of mental calmness and an imbalance in our lifestyles, affecting our mind, body and spirituality.

It is important to become aware of the symptoms of burnout, including feeling tired, let down and purposeless, doubting one's skills and abilities and losing interest in hobbies. If not recognized early, burnout can lead to physical ailments such as headaches, stomach problems, poor digestion, chronic pain and sleeplessness. The key to treating burnout is not to focus solely on the stress factors or to reflexively go to a therapist, but rather to first understand the root cause of the issue and focus on recovering both the mind and body. It can be a vicious cycle. Recognizing the symptoms early is crucial to finding a solution.

Stress is a natural part of life that we all experience. However, it is not necessarily an enemy, as it also teaches us to focus on our mental and physical wellbeing. It reminds us to take breaks when overwhelmed. Although working hard is good, it is equally important to give our body a much-needed balance. Taking a short break is one of the best ways to counter burnout. It helps us realize that our body was tired all this time and needed a recharge. Whether we plan to take a break on a tropical island or visit a neighbouring town, travel can be that much-needed mental reset. However, just travelling in general is not enough to fix burnout. We need to practice mindfulness while travelling.

*"O you who believe, seek help through patience and prayer. Surely, Allah is with those who are patient."* (Qur'an 2:153)

Mindful travelling means removing non-essential tasks from our agenda during travel. It involves focusing on sleep, reading books, seeking social support, talking to friends and slowing down. Mindful travelling activates our repair system. By keeping our attention on the present moment, it prioritizes our health over every other trivial matter of our worldly life. One of the critical points that mindful travelling teaches us is to learn how to rest. It gives us time to work on self-management and simplify our lives without feeling embarrassed.

*"Do not lose heart and do not grieve and you are the upper-most if you are believers."* (Qur'an 3:139)

# Respecting Our Time

*"(I swear) by the Time, man is in a state of loss indeed, except those who believed and did righteous deeds and exhorted each other to follow truth and exhorted each other to observe patience."* (Qur'an 103:1-3)

One of the worst things to do while travelling is checking our work emails; the second worst is endless scrolling on social media, updating statuses and sharing everything we do. It not only shows a lack of respect for our travel companions but also takes away the experience of being in a new place. Unfortunately, in today's world, our phones have become a constant companion. Some travellers even rely on their phones to experience the world. By viewing everything through a small screen, they prefer an inferior substitute to the actual moment itself. Smartphones and cameras take our attention away from what is happening around us. The average person spends up to three hours on screens today and this number is even higher when travelling. We might feel an urge to film everything we see. Soon, the focus goes from the filming down to the camera angle, the resolution quality, hashtags and emojis. Eventually, the entire experience becomes nothing but a social media post and one may only recall their travel destination if they check their social media post to recall that specific vacation. It is important to remember that our travel experiences must be cherished as personal moments that we can hold onto for years to come.

*"...and know that Allah knows whatever is in yourselves, so be wary of Him. And know that Allah is Ever-Forgiving, Ever-Forbearing."* (Qur'an 2:235)

**Digital detox:** Travelling with mindfulness cannot be done without a digital detox. It requires a change in mindset. As travellers, we have a choice to experience everything in its truest form or to record it with our phones and rely on these recordings to remember the trip. It is important to differentiate whether our travel is solely to capture photos for social media or if there is a deeper reason behind it. Mindful photography is also crucial. We need to ask ourselves if a certain photo is necessary or is being taken just for recognition on social media. We should question whether we share too much of our personal life or feel the need to have an audience each time we travel.

Digital detox has become a necessity, especially when we travel with our family and young children. Nowadays, it is more important than ever to be present in the moment rather than just hiding behind the camera. Some people say that they enjoy their experience more when they take fewer pictures and it helps them appreciate the beauty of their surroundings. It creates a clear distinction between what is essential and what is not.

It is important to dissociate from technology while enjoying scenic beauty. Disconnecting and slowing down, along with unplugging from social media, is an excellent way to deactivate those impulses to share everything with the world. By doing this, we can reflect and think more deeply about the experience. For instance, while walking on a glacier, we can imagine how people lived there without what we consider the basic necessities of modern life. Similarly, we can imagine our Muslim ancestors and their lifestyle when visiting historical Islamic sites.

Being in the present moment is important. One way to do it is by keeping away from the phone for at least half a day during travel. Doing so can minimize distractions, leading to a happier and more relaxed state. There is more connection with the present moment when the urge to check social media has been overcome. We should not always be constantly accessible for an unlimited time. Our free time is valuable and should be well spent. Unfortunately, some people travel frequently but spend more than half their trip inside their hotel room, checking their social media or watching television, which prevents them from truly experiencing the joys of travelling.

**Motorized mindfulness:** Psychologists, due to the rampant use of social media, have coined the term "motorized mindfulness," meaning observing details around us while we are on the go. A road trip is an excellent example of motorized mindfulness. Not only is it cheaper than flying, but it also gives us the freedom to go in any direction we choose. We can also stop and explore historical and geological landmarks. When travelling by train, bus or boat, we can observe topography, architecture and nature's details, such as the colours of mountains, the shapes of trees or wildlife. Some also recommend involving the entire group of friends or family in motorized mindfulness by calling out the directions of the sights as they appear, for example, a sea lion at two o'clock or a whale spout at nine o'clock. It is a wholesome experience that can be further enhanced by recalling the *dhikr* of Allah ﷻ, giving us both emotional and spiritual wellbeing.

"The wise person is not unmindful of remembering the Hereafter at any time, as it is his final destination and resting place. In everything he sees of water, fire or anything else, it is a lesson and admonition, for a man looks at things according to his concerns." (Al-Ghazali, Revival of the Religious Sciences, 1/139)

## Mindfulness in Nature

*"It is not for the sun to catch up with the moon, nor does the night outrun the day. each is travelling in an orbit of their own."* (Qur'an 36:40)

To truly call oneself a nature lover, one must immerse oneself in the forest. Bona fide nature lovers walk into the woods and focus on taking deeper breaths and feeling the muscles of their body as they walk. They pay attention to the rustling of the leaves, observe various types of ferns, open up their senses to natural forest scents and enjoy the light drizzle of rain. This is what forest bathing is, i.e., taking in the atmosphere of the forest. The concept of forest bathing is translated from the Japanese term *shinrin-yoku*, which involves taking a meditative walk in the forest, staying in the present moment and appreciating the ambiance of nature around us. However, Almighty Allah ﷻ introduced the concept of forest bathing to us centuries before the rest of the world highlighted its importance. Allah ﷻ has ordered us in the Qur'an to contemplate His Majesty when observing nature. Everything in nature is involved in *dhikr*. As we walk in the woods, it feels as though they all resonate with us in recalling Allah's ﷻ favours upon us. Unfortunately, not many Muslims explore nature, even though Allah ﷻ gave us the example of Prophet

Dawud, who used to remember Allah during his nature walks. His forest bathing technique was deeply spiritual, where he remembered Allah and everything in nature used to join him in doing the *dhikr*.

*"Surely, We bestowed grace on Dawūd from Us: 'O mountains, pronounce with him Allah's purity repeatedly – and you too O birds!' And We made iron soft for him."* (Qur'an 34:10)

Nature walks have a tremendous positive impact on one's health. They promote wellbeing and elevate mood. People who walk in the woods are said to be more relaxed than those who walk only in the city, with lower levels of stress hormones and blood pressure. However, deep contentment from nature comes only when one remembers the Almighty who created nature. For a Muslim, the concept of forest bathing is incomplete if the *dhikr* of Allah is not part of it. While forest bathing and walking in the woods may elate our senses, only spiritual connection can bring tranquility to the soul. The next time we go on a walk, let's focus on absorbing every detail and not just simply noting the beauty and moving on. Observe the vastness of botanical life and its diversity in the forest, the shapes and colours of different leaves, the widely spread roots of the trees at their base and the tall canopy at the top.

***"Have you not seen how Allah has set forth a parable: A good word is like a good tree, having its root firm and its branches in the sky. It brings its fruits at all times with the will of its Lord. Allah sets forth the parables for the people, so that they may take lesson." (Qur'an 14:24-5)***

Allah ﷻ has placed sublime beauty in nature. It is up to us to train our minds to observe the details of nature around us. The next time we travel, let's plan to visit at least one garden or hike one mountain. As we explore, we should observe the colour of the meadows, the surroundings of the hiking trails and the fragrances of the trees. Nature's beauty is such that we don't need to book an expensive trip to enjoy it. A mindful nature walk can be done during our daily commute by taking time to notice the tender shoots along a sidewalk, focusing on the summer breeze or observing the details of self-germinating wildflowers, the time of dawn and the moon's growth and waning each night.

*"He is the One who has made the sun a glow and the moon a light and determined for it stages, so that you may learn the number of the years and the calculation (of time). Allah has not created all this but for a rightful purpose. He elaborates the signs for a people who understand."* (Qur'an 10:5)

## Emotional Decluttering

*"Indeed, there is a lesson in all this for him who has a heart and gives ear (to the truth) attentively."* (Qur'an 50:37)

Our daily routines often feel rushed and calculated, with a set schedule that involves catching up on one task after another. We tend to prioritize getting things done quickly. Slowing down and reducing the speed of our lives is not usually on the agenda. However, slowing down our tasks is essential for our mental and spiritual refreshment. In Islam, there are various ways to slow down and reflect, such as through mandatory daily prayers, recitation of the Qur'an and morning and evening *dhikr*. This is the downtime that Allah ﷻ has given us for self-reflection before moving back into the worldly life as per His guidelines. Nevertheless, modern life still feels rushed due to overwhelming schedules. That's why it's important to make time after *Fajr* prayer to slow down and reflect, even if it may feel uncomfortable at first. In fact, if one wants to develop a new habit while travelling, consider making the post-*Fajr* slowdown a part of one's daily routine.

Simak narrated: "When the Prophet ﷺ observed the dawn prayer, he sat at the place of worship till the sun had risen enough." (Muslim 670b)

After performing the *Fajr* prayer and reciting the Qur'an, we usually have about twenty-five to thirty minutes before sunrise. This time might be too early for breakfast and unsafe for a walk or hike. We also probably have no household responsibilities since we are away. This is the perfect time to sit quietly and reflect on our spiritual health. Instead of focusing on planning the rest of the day, we may contemplate our productivity for *Ākhirah*. Are we too focused on worldly possessions or are we also collecting assets for *Ākhirah*? How often do we remember Allah ﷻ outside of prayer time? Are we consistent with our Qur'an recitation? Are we prepared for the five questions that will be asked in *Ākhirah*?

"The son of Adam will not be dismissed from his Lord on the Day of Resurrection until he is questioned about five matters: his life and how he lived it, his youth and how he spent it, his wealth and how he earned and spent it and how he acted upon his knowledge." (Tirmidhi 2416)

The time after *Fajr* can be a mini spiritual retreat every day, as it reroutes our focus towards what is important. Consequently, we redirect our soul towards the direction of achieving Allah's mercy. It reminds us of the importance of the *Ākhirah*, which can be obscured by worldly distractions that occupy our daily lives. Slowing down from *Fajr* to sunrise is a form of Islamic meditation that helps us snap out of the hustle culture and focus on a single task. As a bonus for Muslims, we not only feel refreshed after this short retreat but are also rewarded for remembering Allah ﷻ. Scholars also recommend making supplications during this time and asking Allah ﷻ to place barakah in our time and let us use it in a way that pleases Him. Starting our day with this new habit makes us feel different and once the habit of the post-*Fajr* slowdown retreat is developed during travel, it becomes easier to practice it in our daily routine back home.

"Religion is easy and whoever overburdens himself in his religion will not be able to continue in that way. So, you should not be extremists but try to be near to perfection and receive the good tidings that you will be rewarded; and gain strength by worshipping in the mornings, the afternoons and during the last hours of the night." (Bukhari 39)

## Gratitude

*"And when man is afflicted by pain, he calls his Lord turning to Him passionately. Thereafter, when He blesses him with some favour from Him, he forgets that for which he was calling Him earlier…"* (Qur'an 39:8)

Gratitude is a precious gem. It holds the power to transform the perception of being less fortunate into a feeling of abundance. Without it, even the wealthiest may remain in a state of unease. To harbor gratitude means valuing Allah's blessings. There is a profound spiritual essence in gratitude, as it connects us with our inner selves and cultivates a positive perspective on life. Those who are grateful are loved by Allah ﷻ.

***"We shall soon reward the grateful." (Qur'an 3:145)***

Being grateful for the many blessings should foster good behaviour and compassion. It boosts energy and inspiration. Our subconscious mind gets trained to notice things we have, rather than wishing for the ones we do not. This imparts a positive psychological benefit to our mind and body by creating a feeling of comfort. Research has shown a lower rate of inflammation and better genetic makeup in people who regularly practice gratitude. Moreover, gratitude has been linked to improved mental health, reducing stress and anxiety. Though gratitude is important in every area of our life, it becomes even more important while we travel and explore the world. The following are some of the ways travel can make us more grateful if we think about this aspect of it.

**To travel is a blessing:** Travel, in general, is an opportunity that allows one to explore the world and see Allah's ﷻ beautiful creations. It is a blessing that requires relatively stable finances and job security, as well as a peaceful home to return to. However, it is important to be appreciative of these things, as they can be taken away at any moment. One must never show ingratitude by disobeying Allah's ﷻ commands, such as prayers, supplications and recitation of the Qur'an. Similarly, it is also important to keep in mind that travel is not a measure of success and it must never spark a flame of pride or arrogance.

> ***"They know something superficial of the worldly life, but of the Hereafter they are negligent." (Qur'an 30:7)***

**A healthy body is a great blessing:** Can we imagine ourselves without feet or not having any vision in our eyes or not being able to drink water and eat food, which is essential for our well-being since birth? Our organs work tirelessly without any cost to us and we often take them for granted. These are all the blessings that we must remember on a daily basis and even more so during travel, as only a healthy body that functions well can take full advantage of travelling and exploring the world.

*"Say, 'He is the One who has originated you and made for you ears and eyes and hearts. How little you pay gratitude!'"* (Qur'an 67:23)

**The blessings at home:** Travel can help us appreciate the blessings we have at home. When away from home, we are in a vulnerable position, both financially and physically. We don't have the security of knowing we will be able to return home safely. Ultimately, it's only Allah سبحانه وتعالى who has the power to bring us back to our home where there is a warm bed to sleep, food to eat and a safe place to live.

"Whoever among you wakes up secure in his property, healthy in his body and has his food for the day, it is as if he were given the entire world." (Tirmidhi 2346)

**Free from materialism:** Travel can be a great way to realize that our happiness does not depend on material possessions. One may feel contented even when camping at the North Pole if there is inner peace, while another may remain sleepless even when staying at a luxury resort. Although everyone desires a comfortable life, travel teaches us that material things are only a source of temporary happiness. True contentment and peace come from connecting with our Creator.

> ***"This worldly life is nothing but amusement and play and the Last Abode is real life indeed. If only they knew!" (Qur'an 29:64)***

**Allah's help on every step:** While travelling, we may sometimes feel as though a higher power comes to the rescue whenever there is a moment of anxiety. We arrive at our destination safe and sound, our luggage remains intact, we do not face any medical emergencies and we are protected from theft and assault. All of this leads us to contemplate Allah's ﷻ help for travellers. It is Allah who makes our journey easier.

*"So, (O mankind and Jinn,) which of the bounties of your Lord will you deny?"* (Qur'an 55:13)

**A medicine for depression**: It has been established that spending time outdoors while travelling can boost optimism and aid in treating depression. However, individuals with mental health issues may benefit more from travelling with a grateful outlook. Practicing gratitude involves being thankful for bodily functions, financial stability and observing other people at the airport or destination to take the focus away from one's own problems. Psychologists have introduced the concept of "slum travel" (to be discussed later in the book), which involves feeling better by learning from the lives of others. Patients with depression are also encouraged to start gratitude journaling while travelling and continue this practice afterward. This activity has been shown to improve positivity and reduce negative thoughts and feelings of emptiness.

*"...and He gave you whatever you asked for. If you (try to) count the bounties of Allah, you cannot count them all. Indeed, man is highly unjust, very ungrateful."* (Qur'an 14:34)

***"In the earth, there are signs for those who (seek truth to) believe and in your own selves! So, do you not perceive?" (Qur'an 51:20-1)***

## Travel Melancholy

In our modern society we tend to have a low tolerance for problems. We sometimes imagine that our lives should always be free of problems, this could be due to people presenting images of perfect lives on social media.

Nowadays, we rarely witness sadness and grief in people's lives, except in a war zone where a society suffers as a whole. As a result, our minds find anything outside our comfort zone unnatural and intolerable. Interestingly, travellers may suffer from all these issues during their journey. It has been reported that travellers abroad for long periods of time experience loneliness and homesickness once the initial excitement is over. They feel detached from their social network and find it difficult to get adjusted to the new culture.

Sometimes the opposite to this happens and travellers feel post-travel blues upon returning home. This is even worse, as they now find it difficult to adjust to their old routine or feel sad that home is not as scenic as the place they travelled to. It's important to remember a few key points here.

**Getting to know ourselves:** Travelling can provide us with valuable perspective on our behaviour, especially when we find ourselves in uncomfortable situations. It allows us to gain a better understanding of how we handle difficult circumstances. This shift in outlook can help us adapt to any change that may come later in life. Moreover, travelling also brings extra time to reflect on our spiritual connection with Allah ﷻ . Have we been too preoccupied with worldly matters or have we also been thinking about the afterlife? Have we spent too much time on social media or have we disconnected from our phones and focused on the present moment?

**Habit check:** Travel also gives us time to evaluate our habits. It helps us stay organized with fewer belongings. It gives us insight into areas where we need to focus on organizing our daily chores. After returning from a trip, we can reflect on any new habits we may have formed and redirect our subconscious mind accordingly.

**Our job is a blessing:** Going back to the scheduled daily routine may seem daunting. However, there are two ways to adopt a positive mindset towards it. First, express gratitude for the stable finances that allow us to travel and see the world. Second, view our work as a blessing and a source of halal income. Having a job means we have the opportunity to save up and travel again if we wish. Our work should be seen as an opportunity, not a source of anxiety.

**Post-travel assessment:** The mindset of a traveller is crucial. If one travels to gain new experiences rather than to escape from daily routine, they are less likely to feel post-travel blues. It's also beneficial to reflect on what could have been improved during the trip to enhance future travel experiences. Even if someone travelled to take a break from their monotonous routine, they could reflect on the opportunity to relax and rejuvenate and appreciate returning to the security of their home.

**Making *du'ā'* after coming home:** Lastly, there are no post-travel blues for those who remain grateful for the blessing of being able to travel and safely return home. They make *du'ā'* for future travels and are less likely to experience negative emotions upon returning home.

# Contemplative Travel

Every traveller sees the world differently. No two experiences can be exactly the same. However, it doesn't mean our experiences cannot be useful to others. Creating a framework of our travel explorations and sharing the details of travel routes, places to visit and events to attend may help others make informed decisions. Similarly, we can also participate in charity work as we explore new destinations. In this section on contemplative travel, we will explore how a Muslim traveller can benefit others through their travels.

## Volunteer Travel

"If anyone relieves a Muslim believer from one of the hardships of this worldly life, Allah will relieve him of one of the hardships of the Day of Resurrection." (Muslim 2699)

Volunteer travel, also known as voluntourism, is a way to combine sightseeing with humanitarian work. Though not a new concept, it became popularized after the establishment of organizations like Red Crescent and Red Cross. Nowadays, many humanitarian organizations offer opportunities to travel and help other people while discovering new places. It is also often recommended by psychologists for patients with depression, as it boosts morale by allowing one to help others. Unfortunately, neo-colonialism (including white supremacy), exploitation (i.e., aid never reaching the poor) and foreign aid dependency has made voluntourism a controversial subject in the recent past. However, a Muslim traveller working with a Muslim charity organization should find it a valuable way to unite the *ummah*. Volunteer travel encourages self-reflection, as one carries out new duties while being part of a group. It brings many opportunities to give *sadaqah*, make new friends and experience a sense of purpose and happiness. Many volunteers continue to participate regularly with their travel groups for years to come.

*"Surely those men who give sadaqah (alms) and those women who give sadaqah and have advanced a good loan to Allah, for them it will be multiplied and for them there is a noble reward."* (Qur'an 57:18)

Similar to volunteer travel is an entity called "slum travel." This is not to be confused with poverty tourism, which can often exploit the communities it visits. Instead, slum travel involves going individually to an underserved area in the world to learn or as a part of one's profession, such as anthropology. Slum travel, like volunteer travel, is beneficial in many ways. First, an insight into a poverty-stricken population opens one's eyes to a new world where people lack many luxuries. We might encounter some unpleasant realities and witness social inequities and injustices. It can be both intriguing and challenging to confront the sad realities of some communities, in terms of weak economy and wealth disparity between the rich and the poor of the same city. Slum travel widens our travel horizon so that travel is not always about checking out beautiful places; it can also let us taste the bitter realities of life on our planet. Currently, slum travelling is popular in several countries of Africa, India, Mexico, Thailand, Indonesia and the Philippines. We may also find slum tours in these countries where a dedicated touring company takes us on a guided tour in a slum area.

*"Surely those who recite Allah's Book and have established salah and have spent, secretly and openly, from what We have provided to them – they hope for a trade that will never crash."* (Qur'an 35:29)

Regardless of our approach, both volunteer and slum travelling can be incredibly beneficial for a Muslim traveller. By closely observing the unpleasant living situation of others, we not only become grateful for the blessings Allah ﷻ has bestowed upon us but also feel privileged to assist those in need. This can be a transformative process for our *iman*, when we meet poor people and help them in any way possible, whether through providing housing, clean water, educational projects or transportation. Any assistance we provide will be counted as *sadaqah* and can pave the way for Allah's ﷻ mercy and Jannah in the *Ākhirah*. These experiences can deepen our understanding of Qur'anic teachings regarding charity and compassion, inspiring us to embody these values in our daily lives.

***"Say, 'Surely, my Lord extends provision for whomsoever He wills and straitens (it) for him. And whatever thing you spend, He replaces it and He is the best of the sustainers.'" (Qur'an 34:39)***

## Documenting our Travel

"Keep a notebook. Travel with it, eat with it, sleep with it.... lead pencil markings endure longer than memory." –Jack London

Nowadays, it is routine to document travels and record them on the go in various ways. However, the preferred method has shifted towards digital documentation and publishing on social media, as opposed to taking notes or turning the travel experience into a book. Both methods can be advantageous, depending on how they are used.

**Digital recording:** Recording travel with a camera can serve multiple purposes, such as creating a personal record or sharing it with immediate friends and family. Additionally, it can be published online for the world to see, potentially earning income. The type of camera gear used varies from person to person, with some preferring digital cameras with image stabilization and tripods, while others opt for shooting videos with their phone or a GoPro camera. Sharing travel experiences digitally has several advantages. It can help promote the Islamic heritage of a place and boost its tourism economy. Short vlogs can also inform others about a journey and what to expect in a certain location. Once online, these videos can continue to be watched by prospective travellers, benefitting others from our experiences. Through vlogs, people can explore sacred places, prophetic towns and other Islamic historical sites from the comfort of their homes, which can be particularly helpful for those who cannot afford to travel. Additionally, we can share the beauty of nature and recall the *dhikr* of Allah ﷻ to gain rewards as we travel. If our videos are made according to Islamic guidelines and the content benefits others, we leave a form of perpetual charity through travel vlogs. However, there are also a few disadvantages to consider.

First, the one making vlogs is at risk of falling into a trap of *Shaytan*. Seeking fame, self-promotion and over-sharing our personal lives to gain an online following can lead to *ujub* (self-boasting), *kibr* (thinking less of others) and *takabbur* (arrogance). Islamic scholars advise against pursuing fame and self-talk as it can lead to pride, making us slaves to our *nafs* and blinding us from differentiating between what is halal and what is not. Some scholars even suggest avoiding taking selfies altogether, as it can be detrimental to our mental wellbeing. While travel photography is allowed in Islam, taking selfies everywhere we go can lead to excessive focus on our self-image, perfectionism, body dissatisfaction and depression. Even the American Psychiatric Association has acknowledged the harms of selfie obsession and recognized it as a mental illness.

*"Remember your Lord in your heart with humility and awe and without speaking loudly, in mornings and evenings and do not be among the heedless."* (Qur'an 7:205)

**Travel journaling:** Journaling is a personal pursuit; however, it brings numerous benefits to travellers. By recording details such as the places we visited, where we stayed, the food we ate, what we did and the things we saw, we can create a lasting memory of our journey. Journaling is an excellent way to reflect on a voyage and can help us keep track of our travel goals and focus on what needs to be accomplished on our trip. These notes can also serve as a helpful reference guide for future travel. Additionally, journaling can be a practical way to keep track of expenses. Some people also use their journals to document their *dhikr* and supplications, as well as track their memorization.

***"Say, 'Travel in the land and look how He has originated the creation. Then Allah will create the subsequent creation. Surely Allah is powerful to do everything.'" (Qur'an 29:20)***

**Travel writing:** Muslim travellers of the past had a unique way of documenting their travels that differed significantly from current explorers. The documentation process was digitized over time and as a result, there are very few travel writings authored by Muslim travellers today. However, in medieval times, travel writing was a major literary genre among Muslims, especially Arabs and some of the finest travel writers in history emerged from this period. Travel memoirs authored by Ibn Jubayr, Ibn Battuta and Ibn Khaldun are still widely read today. They used the travel genre to describe the state of the Muslim community during their respective times, combining actual and spiritual properties. Later, Al-Tahtawi, Al-Shidyaq and other writers expanded this genre to include documentation of other cultures around the world. Muslim travel writings were known for their inspiration and deeper understanding. Writers documented their journeys in such a way that their writings never became outdated, transporting their readers to their era and helping them understand its beauty, history and culture.

***"Man is but a tale after his death. So, be a good tale for whoever should remember." (Ibn Duraid, Kitab al-Maqsurah)***

Unfortunately, the tradition of Muslim travel writing is not being followed as it should be. The younger generation is oblivious to what was once a priority of Muslim travellers. Even when Muslim travellers do write about their journeys, they often lack a spiritual perspective and focus more on secular or personal experiences. However, we can make a difference and continue the tradition of medieval Muslim scholars by writing about our travels. Here are some suggestions:

1. Take note of the historical significance of the places and learn about notable figures from the area.

2. Highlight geological and scientific details from the journey.

3. Collect information about cultural and intercultural practices.

By doing so, we can create a resource that benefits other Muslim travellers materially and spiritually. People may also be inspired to rekindle their relationship with Islamic heritage. Our travel writing can become a valuable guidebook for future generations, just like the work of our pious ancestors.

*"Whoever comes up with good on his own, then Allah is Appreciating, All-Knowing."* (Qur'an 2:158)

*"Allah is well-aware of what you do."* (Qur'an 58:11)

## Helping Others with Experience

*"Help each other in righteousness and piety and do not help each other in sin and aggression."* (Qur'an 5:2)

One of the most incredible things about travel is that it brings an extra boost to one's experience in life. It provides us with knowledge about new cultures and geography and it helps us to develop new planning and budgeting skills. We can use this knowledge to assist others who share our passion for travel. We can create travel plans for them by identifying their priorities and goals for their journey. This can be a fun and exciting hobby, as it allows us to focus entirely on someone else's travel needs and desires.

We may get an opportunity to plan our cousin's next family trip to Dubai or suggest literary destinations in Morocco. We can help people plan their trips even if we have not visited the destination ourselves. By learning about their travel preferences, we can suggest destinations and activities that they will enjoy. People are highly appreciative when we make their travelling seem exciting and beneficial at the same time.

As Muslims, we can also share our knowledge of Islamic laws and customs that may make travel more manageable for other Muslim travellers. We can teach them about the method of *tayammum*, praying *qasr* and other important practices. Additionally, we can create Muslim travel applications and helpful blogs that focus on Islamic civilization, archaeology and architecture. By doing so, we can help other Muslims have a more meaningful and fulfilling travel experience.

*"And seek the (betterment of) the Ultimate Abode with what Allah has given to you and do not neglect your share from this world and do good as Allah did good to you and do not seek to make mischief in the land."* (Qur'an 28:77)

**Failed trips:** As travellers, there will be times when a particular trip does not go as planned. A national park tour might be conducted in a foreign language, the hotel might be a third-class motel, a safari tour might turn out to be online spam and so on. Making mistakes and failing to achieve specific goals are common during travel and are lessons in disguise. Sometimes travellers take that as a failure on their part. They feel guilty and ashamed to talk about it. Regardless of how one thinks about a failed experience, it is much more liberating when one lifts the curtain of supposed failure and finds an opportunity to share it with others. Getting comfortable with the uncomfortable is the key. Acknowledging our mistakes helps us move on and learn from them. After a few years, a failed trip may become a funny anecdote. Moreover, sharing our experiences with others turns them into teachable moments for ourselves and others.

A failed trip helps us set priorities right and deal with uncomfortable situations more calmly. It prepares us for future trips and we learn to be more grateful when things do go as planned. We understand that everything happens according to Allah's decree, which is always for our betterment. As a result, we share our experiences with others so they can learn from them.

> ***"It could be that you dislike something, when it is good for you; and it could be that you like something when it is bad for you. Allah knows and you do not know." (Qur'an 2:216)***

# Solo Travel as a Muslim

Solo travel is an incredibly liberating experience, as it gives travellers the freedom to create their schedules and pursue their interests without any external influences. It allows them to venture out on adventurous expeditions without explaining their choices to anyone. In addition, solo travel can also offer a valuable opportunity for self-reflection and personal growth. It helps to develop problem-solving skills and enables individuals to identify their weaknesses. In this section, we will explore various ways Muslim travellers can make the most of solo travel.

## Solo Specifics for a Muslim

*"Surely, in the creation of the heavens and the earth and in the alternation of night and day, there are signs for the people of wisdom, who remember Allah standing and sitting and (lying) on their sides and ponder on the creation of the heavens and the earth…"* (Qur'an 3:191)

One of the perks of travelling in the modern era is that travelling solo has become more accessible and doable compared with the past. Back in the day, when Ibn Battuta travelled, going solo was dreadful. The long journeys involved riding on animals for days and protecting oneself from desert bandits. Today airports and other public transportation are exceedingly safe. Nonetheless, travellers' lives are still not risk-free.

Solo travel is also becoming increasingly popular among modern-day Muslim explorers. Young Muslim graduates often take time off for vacations and embark on journeys to explore new landscapes. It not only boosts confidence but also adds a fresh perspective to one's thinking and improves mental wellbeing. Solo travelling also provides valuable life experience when tackling challenges on one's own. Hence, it is particularly preferred by outdoor enthusiasts who like to camp in unusual weather conditions in the wilderness, such as staying overnight in an igloo or camping in the Amazonian basin. However, for any Muslim who wants to travel solo, it is important to remember some key points.

**Staying vigilant:** Travelling alone is relatively safe in today's era as long as one remains vigilant about one's surroundings and takes basic precautions. It is important to assess the safety of the destination and the current political and geographical climate during the planning stages of a trip. For example, it may be unsafe to travel if there are riots or forest fires in the area. It is also crucial to ensure that emergency help and mobile phone services are available if one is going backcountry. Experienced travellers rely on their instincts and if a place seems unsafe, it is likely dangerous for a solo traveller. Likewise, one must also be cautious about choosing accommodation. It is better to avoid places that are too cheap or located in suspicious areas where safety may be compromised. Additionally, it is advisable to avoid drawing unnecessary attention to oneself by displaying expensive cameras or branded clothing. As Muslims, we have faith in Allah ﷻ, but we are also responsible for taking precautions, as the Prophet ﷺ advised his companion to tie his camel and then trust in Allah (Tirmidhi 2517).

**Travelling in daylight**: Travelling during the day is much safer than travelling at night. Despite modern advances, night-time journeys are still not free from danger. A traveller is vulnerable to becoming an easy target for criminals who operate at night. The Prophet ﷺ emphasized the risks of travelling alone at night when he said, "If the people knew what I know about travelling alone, then nobody would travel alone at night" (Bukhari 2998). Therefore, it is always advisable to arrive at your destination during daylight hours, especially when travelling alone.

**Group tours:** Group tours can be a great way to explore a place and learn about its history. Although solo travelling has its own charm, group tours provide an opportunity to socialize with fellow travellers and get to know the topography of the area. Many local museums and historical societies offer walking tours, some of which can be very engaging. During the tour, we can make new friends and discover new places to add to our itinerary.

**Avoid complaining**: As a solo traveller exploring the world, things may not always go according to plan. The extraordinary outdoor park on the web may not be scenic in person, leaving one feeling disappointed about wasting time and money. One may even feel homesick and miss the comforts of home. Nevertheless, a lack of comfort or certainty does not mean that the trip is a waste. Solo travel is a choice that makes people more confident in their decision-making skills. Sometimes people may assume that solo travellers are lonely or sad but being comfortable in your own company is the key to enjoying your trip. Our time during solo travel may not be ideal; there can be a moment when the food is not delicious or the hotel room does not meet our expectations. We may even encounter racism or discrimination based on our religion. However, these experiences are teaching moments that help us learn about our capabilities.

> ***"In Allah you must place your trust, if you are believers." (Qur'an 5:23)***

**Practice *tawakkul*:** Solo travelling is a learning opportunity at many levels, but most importantly, it teaches us how to have *tawakkul* in Allah. When travelling solo, we are responsible for dealing with any unforeseen issues that arise on our journey. However, the journey is a beautiful metaphorical depiction of our life in the Hereafter. We are like travellers in this world, sent here with a purpose. When we encounter difficulties, we turn to Allah ﷻ for help, just as a traveller in a foreign place would. That is why the *du'ā'* of a traveller gets accepted, because a traveller is in a vulnerable position, away from home and loved ones. Allah ﷻ is our primary support, as always, but we comprehend it in its truest sense when we travel solo and encounter problems.

*"If Allah helps you, there is none to overcome you. And if He abandons you, then, who is there to help you after that? In Allah the believers should place their trust."* (Qur'an 3:160)

## Muslim Women's Solo Travel

*"...and do not display (your) beauty as it used to be displayed in the days of earlier ignorance."* (Qur'an 33:33)

The topic of solo travel for Muslim women is a highly debated topic among Muslim youth and scholars alike. There are two opinions on this matter. One group of scholars quote hadiths where people asked the Prophet ﷺ about Muslim women's solo travelling, specifying the number of days in their query. The Prophet ﷺ replied, "It is not permissible for a woman who believes in Allah and the Last Day to travel for one day and night except with a *mahram*" (Bukhari 1088). The other group of scholars argue that this hadith was based on the danger of arduous desert journeys in Arabia at that time and that travelling is safe nowadays. They support their arguments with another authentic hadith where the Prophet ﷺ said, "A day will come when a woman will travel from Hira to the Ka'ba, fearing nothing but Allah alone" (Bukhari 3595). Therefore, this group of scholars argues that it is permissible for a woman to travel solo as long as her safety is ensured, such as in public transport and so on. However, regardless of the opinions, scholars have a universal consensus that a woman can travel alone or commute within the city where she lives. The limit of a city or town is applied here since the defined distance is not mentioned. Following are some helpful key points that a Muslim woman can consider when she decides to go on a solo exploration of her surroundings.

"You (women) have been allowed to go out for your needs." (Bukhari 4795)

**Rethink your 'why':** It is important for Muslim women, just like any other traveller, to reflect on their intentions when exploring their locality. Are they using social media to showcase their abilities to others or are they using it to learn and broaden their horizons? Any action taken on social media to impress others can be damaging to our souls, as it falls under ostentation and showing off, which is strongly discouraged in Islam.

***"Say, 'My prayer, my offering, my life and my death are for Allah, the Lord of all the worlds.'" (Qur'an 6:162)***

**Ensure your safety:** Taking a trip alone in a city can be a refreshing experience. However, even if a woman is seeing her hometown, she must be careful regarding basic principles of security. She must avoid disclosing to strangers that she is on her own. Similarly, exhibiting a lack of confidence in finding her route may jeopardize her safety. A group tour with friends and neighbours is always a good idea if one is uncomfortable with solo exploration. Remember that trips do not have to be glamorous like what we often see on social media; rather, they become more spiritually productive with meaningful conversations. A morning walk with a neighbour or a quiet moment with a cup of tea at a local café can also be a refreshing break.

**Learn as you go:** Solo exploration of one's local area can be highly beneficial if one plans it well. There are many places to visit, such as botanical gardens, historical societies, gardens, local museums and libraries. Even a small rural village may have something unique that sets it apart from other places. Whether the area is known for its organic farming or archaeology, it is worth researching. Additionally, one can join book clubs and other social clubs exclusively for women at libraries, garden centers and museums and even volunteer with them.

**Be the travel guru:** Women who are unable to travel for any reason can offer remote support to other travellers by becoming a travel coach. They can help visitors to their town by sharing their knowledge of the must-see places, local eateries, women-owned businesses and social causes that require attention. This can have a positive impact on the local economy by increasing opportunities for tourism. Additionally, through their travel blogs, women can inspire others who may feel lonely or disconnected in urban settings to explore and appreciate their surroundings.

*"They ask you as to what they should spend. Say: 'Whatever good you spend should be for parents, kinsmen orphans, the needy and the* traveller; *and whatever good you do, Allah is all-aware of it.'"* (Qur'an 2:215)

**Explore with kids:** While it may seem challenging to raise children and travel, motherhood can provide a sense of purpose and meaning to life. Introducing new and exciting activities to the little ones can be an excellent opportunity for learning and growth for everyone involved. For instance, a mother can take her young children for a walk in the woods, where she can teach them about different types of trees and shrubs. Children who learn to observe and appreciate the details of their environment tend to grow up to be helpful citizens of their community. Additionally, a mother can plan a picnic, an outdoor book club or a nature hike with her children, providing a unique and memorable experience for all.

***"Each of you is a shepherd and each of you is responsible for his flock." (Abu Dawud 2928)***

## Daily Work Commute

"Take account of yourselves before it is taken of you. Weigh your deeds before they are weighed for you (i.e. on the day of judgement) and beautify yourselves (with good deeds) for the great display (on the day of judgement)." (Umar ibn al-Khattab)

Enduring long work commutes is a part of modern-day living, especially in bigger cities. According to an estimate, up to 60% of people drive to work and their daily commute may range from twenty-seven minutes to two hours.[1] Traffic, roadblocks and construction can cause further delays. Whether in one's car or on public transport such as a bus or subway, commuting can dissipate our time and energy. Nevertheless, it can also be an opportunity to gain knowledge and earn rewards. For Muslims, daily commutes are an excellent opportunity for various reasons. Here are some tips on how to take maximum advantage of this time.

**Bonding with the Qur'an:** The Qur'an is our travel guidebook in this journey of life. Unfortunately, many of us believe we can have a safe journey without opening the instruction manual. Our daily commute brings an excellent opportunity to listen to the Qur'an (with translation when one does not understand Arabic), appreciate its commentary and even memorize an *ayah* or *surah*. The Prophet ﷺ said that one feels envious of the one who keeps himself busy with the Qur'an (Bukhari 7528). The path of Jannah gets easier for the one who tries to gain knowledge of the Qur'an. People who often read the Qur'an will stand among the beloved angels of Allah in the Hereafter (Muslim 1862).

Anas ibn Malik reported that the Prophet ﷺ said, "Verily, Allah has His people among humanity." They asked, "O Prophet of Allah, who are they?" The Prophet ﷺ said, "They are the people of the Qur'an, the people of Allah and His chosen ones." (Ibn Majah 215)

**Listening to Islamic lectures:** Listening to Islamic lectures is a great way to utilize commute time effectively. One can listen to the talks and classes of scholars on topics that have been on the wish list for a long time. This could include any bayan on Islamic law or any topic related to the current social issues of Muslims. The more we listen to Islamic speeches, the more knowledge of deen we can gain.

***"And whoever believes in Allah, He guides his heart." (Qur'an 64:11)***

**Read books and watch educational lectures:** If a commute involves public transportation, one can utilize this time to read more books and watch educational sessions. We should take up the habit of reading seriously and develop a passion for it. It is a necessity for a healthy brain and helps us gain wisdom.

*"My Lord, advance me in knowledge."* (Qur'an 20:114)

**Reflect on the journey:** Firstly, look around and notice the creations of Allah ﷻ, such as the mountains, rivers, birds and even the structures made by humans, all of which are the result of knowledge given by Allah ﷻ. Secondly, remember that only Allah can take us to our destination. As travellers, we may commute to work without much thought, but death could happen at any moment. Therefore, arriving safely at our destination is a blessing in itself.

*"And He is with you wherever you are."* (Qur'an 57:4)

- Make sure documents are also saved in your email, maybe as drafts.
- Pack light, leaving some room for shopping.
- Arrive in daylight.
- Stay in touch with one or two family members back home.
- Ask the hotel staff about unsafe areas.
- Save the numbers of the places where you stay.
- Stay alert and be wary of people who try to be over-friendly.

# Staycation

The relentless pace of our lives can make us feel that there is no time to handle anything. This is when it is crucial to surrender our control and take a vacation in which we do nothing, not even go out: a staycation. Staying at home during vacation time is not a new idea, but to do so consciously is becoming more popular due to hectic schedules, increasing burnout rates and the expense of travel. In this section, we will explore some of the best ways to enjoy a staycation and how we can make it beneficial for our *Ākhirah*.

## Staycation, Still a Good Option

*"Allah has made your houses a place of comfort for you."* (Qur'an 16:80)

The results-oriented mindset has forced a schedule-driven lifestyle. People focus on the future, preventing them from enjoying the present moment. A dismal reality of current times is that people tend to put off things until the perfect moment arrives, i.e., seeing nature in its perfect form or having the most scenic drive, instead of enjoying the flowers that bloom in our backyards. The same goes for travel, where people often overlook the beauty of their own neighbourhoods while chasing exotic locations and foreign landscapes. To avoid the financial burden of travel expenses, many people have embraced the concept of the staycation. It is a time to enjoy our homes and cherish what we have rather than constantly seeking out new destinations.

> ***"You lack a foot to travel?***
> ***Then journey into yourself" - Rumi***

**Staycation ≠ laziness:** The term "staycation" is sometimes associated with laziness and frugality. For Muslim families, it can even be seen as a form of oppression, as one may misinterpret that the families are not allowed to go out together or not let their women have a vacation. The concept of staycation, however, is gaining popularity in many Western countries. It is because we often lead busy lives where our schedules must always be occupied. To counter this, a staycation reassures us that we don't always need to have something on the agenda for the day. It allows us some free time without feeling guilty about not having anything planned. A staycation can be a time to reflect on how we may choose to spend our time and be more flexible with our daily routine. We may go for a short daytrip in the morning or take a professional course in the evening, all while doing our daily chores at a more relaxed pace. However, it can have a negative impact if one stays in bed all day or watches television for hours. Staycation is not just a chance to catch up on cleaning or reorganizing. It is our time to explore our surroundings as if we were tourists and catch up with family and friends.

"O Allah, I seek refuge with You from helplessness, laziness, cowardice and feeble old age; I seek refuge with You from afflictions of life and death and seek refuge with You from the punishment in the grave." (Bukhari 2823)

**Take a rest:** We are told that we have to stay constantly busy to achieve success. Our society seems to reward those who sleep less and work more. However, life need not be this way. Allah ﷻ has taught us to recuperate and focus on a single task every few hours in the form of prayers. The Prophet ﷺ also demonstrated a mindful daily routine that included time for *dhikr*, ibadah, social life, teaching, visiting the sick, accepting invitations, rest and self-care. Hence, we must reintroduce the concept of rest into our lives.

> ***"Your body has a right over you..." (Bukhari 5199)***

**Productive staycation:** Being at home during a staycation does not mean neglecting household chores. Instead, it is the overloading of the to-do list that must be avoided. We might find it more enjoyable and productive to choose just one project or task at a time. One might feel guilty for the empty hours on the schedule – however, the short breaks during staycation help us restore focus for the tasks that require concentration later. A staycation can have different meanings for different people, as we all have unique preferences when it comes to our downtime choices. Whether we like to spend time with loved ones, explore hobbies, visit museums or take a walk in the park, a transitory vacation in our hometown helps us recharge our batteries and refocus on our priorities.

**Staycation with children:** Planning a staycation with your children can be a great way to spend quality time together and improve their lifestyle habits in a fun and engaging way, especially if their routine lives do not allow for it otherwise. Starting with food preparation, they can actively be involved in the kitchen during mealtimes. This can help enhance their fine motor skills, teach them how to follow directions and allow them to observe baking and cooking. Their involvement in the tasks depends on their age. For example, younger children between the ages of three and five can help with tasks such as tearing greens, stirring, mushing and squeezing. They can also help serve plates. Children between five and nine can help add spices and pod beans and pour liquids from containers. Children above nine can help (with supervision) with blending, stirring, microwaving and meal planning. At the time of the meal, children can be reminded about the source of food and how Allah made it easier for us to do grocery shopping and prepare food at home. It will inculcate a grateful attitude, improving their mental wellbeing over time.

**Minimize screentime**: Staycationing with children means reducing time spent on screens, not vice versa. Zoning out on television (or any screen) slows down brain activity, eventually harming our intellect and cognition. Engaging in natural activities, such as gardening, nature walks and outdoor play, is highly recommended instead of excessive screen time. Close observation of the details of the environment keeps our senses sharp and refreshes our minds simultaneously. For example, going for a walk in the neighbourhood with a book on tree identification can be a great way to engage with children and help them learn about the trees in their surroundings. Parents can also arrange a short day-trip for their children and their friends and set up small workshops to teach outdoor skills, such as knotting, upcycling, foraging, first aid and so on.

**Whatever you do, be honest:** Being authentic in everything we do, including our travelling or staycationing, is important. Trying to fit in with others can often lead to disappointment, as everyone has their own preferences and tastes. We may know someone who is a trendsetter, going on vacation retreats, exploring the national parks or inspiring others through linguistics and spirituality. However, what suits them may not serve us. It is unhelpful to compare our inside with everyone else's outside. That is what staycation teaches us: to develop a bond with our wellbeing. It helps us become more emotionally controlled, thus leading to greater contentment and appreciation for the blessings we have been given by Allah.

*"This worldly life is nothing but amusement and play and the Last Abode is real life indeed. If only they knew!"* (Qur'an 29:64)

- Discover what is required to make our worldly life, as well as our *Ākhirah*, better.
- Focus on how you spend the afternoons. Accept the mistake of wasting time and move on.
- Try to craft manageable to-do lists. The purpose of a staycation is to relax, not to tackle every pending task.
- Do mental and physically challenging chores earlier in the day, so the afternoon is left for relaxation.
- Sleep earlier than regular days, so the body feels rested.

# The Harms of Over-Travelling for a Muslim

Abu Hurairah reported that the Prophet ﷺ said, "Travelling is a torment because it deprives a traveller of his food, drink and sleep. So, when one of you has accomplished his purpose of the journey, let him return home quickly." (Riyad as-Salihin 984)

***"And those who are saved from the greed of their hearts are the successful." (Qur'an 59:9)***

As more people travel the world and explore the outdoors, there is an emerging trend of "over-travelling," especially by almost nomadic travellers, people who travel for months in the name of adventure and exploration. Their travel involves movement from place to place for an extended period of time and the traveller either lives in a van and drives around or flies from one destination to another. Over-travellers brag that they "never get tired of seeing more," but there can be some hidden disadvantages and harms, particularly for Muslim travellers. Here are some examples of how it can adversely affect their lives.

**Material goals**: One should first ascertain one's intention for travelling. Those who travel for knowledge achieve different goals than the ones who explore to gain fame and attention. Travel intended to secure part of the *dunya* is harmful since it comes from the desires of the *nafs*, the lower self. The *nafs* may drive one to keep travelling and if not careful, its inexhaustible desires can throw one into a dungeon of *ghaflah*, where one forgets the real purpose of being alive. Worldly travel for fun and adventure, no matter how enjoyable, seldom gives time to pray with focus as one does at home, nor does it give ample time to recite the Qur'an or learn tafsir. Thus, superficial impulses, when unchecked, can disrupt one's ultimate goal of *Ākhirah*.

"The Hellfire is surrounded by all kinds of desires and passions, while Paradise is surrounded by all kinds of disliked and undesirable things." (Bukhari 6487)

**Ignoring responsibilities**: Over-travelling can make one neglect duties at home. Nowadays, it is not uncommon to encounter social media celebutantes exploring the world for months without checking on their families. Immoderate travel can cause them to disregard the domestic responsibilities entrusted to them by Allah.

**The window of sins:** During religious travel, a traveller's mind is often engaged in *dhikr* and du'a' during their journey. However, it may not be the same when journeying to seek adventure and fun. Excessive leisure travel often involves hopping in and out of airports, hotels and gas stations and it may leave one more prone to heedlessness and *ghaflah*, especially when it comes to the sins of the eyes and the ears. Scholars often regard the eyes and the ears as the windows of sins, because life in current times exposes us to sins through those the most. Modern-day travel, along with its ease and convenience, is a test for our *taqwā*. Sometimes it is difficult to avoid the sinning of the ears (with music playing at restaurants, airports and so on) or the eyes (inappropriate dressing of the opposite gender or explicit content on billboards). It is said that if there is a possibility that travel could lead to the loss of one's faith (by sinning), then it is better to return home and avoid such risks.

*"Then, can one who holds on to a clear proof from his Lord be like those for whom their evil deeds are beautified and who followed their desires?"* (Qur'an 47:14)

**Compromised diet:** People who travel excessively are at risk of contracting food-borne illnesses. There are also risks of water contamination and hygiene-related issues. Travellers rely on others for food and thus struggle to make clean choices every time. A Muslim traveller is at risk, especially outside of the Muslim world, of ingesting food contaminated with what is impermissible.

***"He is the One who has made the earth subjugated for you, so walk on its shoulders and eat out of His provision and to Him is the Resurrection." (Qur'an 67:15)***

**No time to self-reflect:** A habitual traveller might have ways to make time for self-reflection on a journey. Excessive travel, though, can sometimes leave less time for self-reflection. It may inculcate a subliminal seeking of constant gratification and chasing quick wins, leading one to burnout and exhaustion. That is when one needs to slow down and reflect on the purpose of their travel. Is it done to learn something new or is it a chase after an adrenaline rush? The meaning of life is lost if we are always searching for the next purchase, the next holiday destination or the next feel-good experience.

Abdullah ibn Masud narrated that the Prophet ﷺ said, "Whoever transforms all of his concerns into one concern only – the hereafter – Allah will satisfy his demands and needs in this life. As for he who devotes his concerns to worldly matters, Allah will not care in which valley he perishes." (Ibn Majah 4106)

**Chasing happiness:** At times, long-term travel to multiple places is done to make oneself feel happy or at least to avoid some sadness. In the long run, it can lead to a mindset where one is dependent on seeking happiness from material things, often resulting in little to no satisfaction from it in the long run. One may enjoy a long journey, try new cuisines, buy unique souvenirs and take more vacations, but the moments of joy eventually wear off. They mistake pleasure for happiness. Enjoyment is temporary if it is dependent on external factors. True happiness comes from stillness and moderation. It comes from having a connection with the Creator and recognizing one's purpose. A meaningful purpose that serves others and connects us with Allah ﷻ is what defines our happiness in this fleeting life.

*"Never stretch your eyes towards the things We have given to some groups of them to enjoy, so that We put them to test thereby, it being merely glamour of the worldly life. And the bounty of your Lord is much better and more lasting."* (Qur'an 20:131)

*"If you express gratitude, I shall certainly give you more and if you are ungrateful, then My punishment is severe."* (Qur'an 14:7)

**Attracting jealousy**: Travelling for leisure is viewed as a luxury and a sign of opulence and so it can inspire jealousy from others who may feel discontented with their lack of travel opportunities. The whisper of jealousy has been present in humankind since near the beginning, but the rise of social media has made it run rampant. In a fast-paced world where there is constant showcasing of one's "best life", it is natural for people to see travelling as a competition. However, it is important to remember that jealousy can be dangerous, as it can destroy good deeds and lead to negative consequences. The Prophet ﷺ warned us about the dangers of jealousy, stating that it can destroy good deeds just as fire destroys wood (Ibn Majah 4210). The one resentful of others' travel, name and fame is like someone who has an objection to Allah's ﷻ decree. Jealousy is a part of human nature, but displaying it is not. A lowly person shows his envy, while a believer suppresses it.

*"Do not crave something in which Allah has made some of you superior to others. For men there is a share of what they earned and for women, a share of what they earned. Pray to Allah for His grace. Surely, Allah is All-Aware of everything."* (Qur'an 4:32)

*"And do not turn your face away from people and do not walk on the earth haughtily. Surely, Allah does not like anyone who is arrogant, proud."* (Qur'an 31:18)

**Competition:** Travelling is often seen as a competition, where everyone tries to outdo each other by visiting more places and gaining more fame. But this is a never-ending cycle that can lead to negative feelings. Instead of comparing ourselves to others, we should let them inspire us with their positive energy and blessings. We can pray to Allah ﷻ to grant us similar things if it's good for us.

*"Whoever intends (to have) the harvest of the Hereafter, We will increase in his harvest; and whoever intends (to have) the harvest of the world (only), We will give him thereof, while in the Hereafter he will have no share."* (Qur'an 42:20)

**Death is inevitable:** Scholars advise that we should not fear death but fear the state in which we die. Life is at risk for a traveller, whether up in the air or driving a vehicle; any moment may become the last one. Additionally, there is a risk of missing prayers. It would be a significant loss if one dies while travelling for fun, listening to music and ignoring prayers. Someone rightly said that one must visit every place as if it is the last time they are seeing it. It is also important to meet religious people along the way to stay mindful of Akhirah. The Prophet ﷺ used to pray, *"O Allah, let not worldly affairs be our principal concern, nor the ultimate limit of our knowledge and let not those rule over us who do not show mercy to us"* (*Riyad as-Salihin* 833).

> ***"The day they will see it, it will seem to them as if they did not live (in the world) but only for one afternoon or for the morning thereof." (Qur'an 79:46)***

- Happiness is not in a location. *We* are our true home and no amount of travel can satisfy the one who is not contented with oneself.
- Try to control the hunger for appreciation and fame by not posting our beautiful photos on social media.
- Content yourself with letting go of travel plans sometimes, just to shut the door of impulsive pleasure and bring self-control to our emotions.
- Accept life as it is. Our life is a journey that can end at any time. We must live according to our reality and not run after an envisioned ideal life.

# Conclusion

*"Do not be like those who forgot Allah, so He made them forget their own selves."* (Qur'an 59:19)

Travel is a blessing from Allah ﷻ. It widens our horizon and broadens our experience in life. However, why we travel, how we travel and how long we travel for is important. Someone who travels the world but is neglectful of Allah's ﷻ remembrance is like a resentful soul who wastes time chasing fleeting desires, whereas the one who remembers Allah ﷻ and follows His commands earns rewards even when fulfilling goals of worldly life. Our hearts do not have space for both the Creator and the created at the same time. Real happiness is with the Creator and when we seek Him, we remain satisfied with what we have and live a contented life we do not have to run away from.

*"(As for an obedient man, it will be said to him,) 'O contented soul, come back to your Lord, well-pleased, well-pleasing. So, enter among My (special) servants and enter My Paradise.'"* (Qur'an 89:27-30)

"Remember your contemporaries who have passed away and were your age. Remember the honours and fame they earned, the high posts they held and the beautiful bodies they possessed. Today, all of them are turned into dust. They have left orphans and widows behind them, their wealth is being wasted and their houses turned into ruins. No sign of them is left today and they lie in dark holes underneath the earth. Picture their faces before your mind's eye and ponder." (Al-Ghazali)

WORKBOOK

# Before the Trip

My next travel destination is...

I have decided to visit this place because...

My aim from this travel is to...

My anticipation about this place is...

# Packing List

## Documents

- ○ Confirmations/reservations
- ○ Health insurance card
- ○ Rental car information
- ○ Driver's license
- ○ Passport / ID card
- ○ Tickets / itinerary

## Toiletries

- ○ Toothbrush / toothpaste
- ○ Shampoo / conditioner
- ○ Deodorant / roll-on
- ○ Dental floss
- ○ Razor / shaving cream
- ○ Nail file / nail cutter
- ○ Hairbrush / comb
- ○ Make-up
- ○ Moisturizer / cream
- ○ Feminine hygiene
- ○ Cotton swabs

## Literary

- ○ Travel journal
- ○ Books
- ○ Children's books
- ○ Travel guide
- ○ Hiking maps

## Prayer Items

- ○ Travel prayer mat
- ○ Prayer beads
- ○ Prayer shawl / jilbab
- ○ Travel Qur'an

## Clothing

- ○ T – shirts / shirts
- ○ Pants
- ○ Sweaters
- ○ Jacket
- ○ Raincoat
- ○ Shoes / boots
- ○ Sandals
- ○ Socks

## Additional Items

- ○ Sunscreen
- ○ Notebook / pen
- ○ Mobile /camera chargers
- ○ Vitamins
- ○ Travel first-aid kit
- ○ ..........
- ○ ..........
- ○ ..........
- ○ ..........
- ○ ..........
- ○ ..........
- ○ ..........
- ○ ..........
- ○ ..........
- ○ ..........
- ○ Umbrella
- ○ Insect repellant
- ○ Hat / gloves
- ○ Laundry bag
- ○ Green tea / herbal tea
- ○ ..........
- ○ ..........
- ○ ..........
- ○ ..........
- ○ ..........
- ○ ..........
- ○ ..........
- ○ ..........
- ○ ..........
- ○ ..........

# Transport Log

| Mode | Terminal | Date/Time | Confirmation Number |
| --- | --- | --- | --- |
| Flight / Train / Bus | | | |
| Rental Car | | | |
| | | | |

# Accommodation

| Location | Hours | Check in Date/Time | Notes |
| --- | --- | --- | --- |
| | | | |

# Restaurants

| Location | Hours | Distance | Notes |
| --- | --- | --- | --- |
| | | | |
| | | | |
| | | | |
| | | | |

# Islamic Centers

| Location | Hours | Phone Number | Notes |
| --- | --- | --- | --- |
| | | | |
| | | | |
| | | | |
| | | | |
| | | | |

# Bucket list

*Suggestions: museums, historical sites, bookstores and libraries, botanical gardens, national and state parks, zoos, aquariums, and safaris.*

| Location | Hours | Tickets | Notes |
|---|---|---|---|
| | | | |
| | | | |
| | | | |
| | | | |

# Tours and Trips

| Location | Hours | Tickets | Notes |
|---|---|---|---|
| | | | |
| | | | |
| | | | |
| | | | |

# After the Trip

How has this trip changed my understanding of this part of the world

What else do I want to see if I ever come here again?

What was the best moment on this trip?

Where am I going next on my adventure?

# Questions for Reflection

What did I learn about myself on this trip?

How can I make myself better in my deen?

How did this trip help me with my deen?

Did I stay connected with Allah during my journey?

What do I need to do to improve my ibaadah?

# Notes

# Bibliography

## Part 1: Travel in Islam – A Brief History

1. Richard M. Eaton, "Islamic history as global history," in Michael Adas, ed., Islamic and European Expansion: The Foraging of a Global Order. Philadelphia: Temple University Press, 1993,12.
2. Hassam Munir, "How Islam Spread Throughout the World," (Yaqeen Institute), 2020, retrieved from https://yaqeeninstitute.org/read/paper/how-islam-spread-throughout-the-world#ftnt4
3. Abd al-Wahid Dhanun Taha, "The Historical Process of the Spread of Islam," in the Different aspects of Islamic culture, vol 3: The spread of Islam throughout the world, eds. Idris al-Hareir and Al-Hadji Ravane M'Baye. Paris: UNESCO, 2011:134
4. Rakhym Beknazarov, "Analyzing the Spread of Islam in Western Kazakhastan through Architectural Monuments," Anthropology of the Middle East 3, no.1, Spring 2008:35.
5. Muslim Heritage, Discover the Golden Age of Muslim Civilization, (Muslim Heritage), 2020, retrieved from

https://muslimheritage.com/people/scholars/ibn-said-al-maghribi/

6. "The Slavs of al-Ya'qubi's The Book of Countries and of the History." (Jassa), 2016, retrieved from https://www.jassa.org/?p=7188
7. Al-Muqaddasi. *The Best Divisions for Knowledge of the Regions: A Translation of Ahsan al-taqasim fi ma'rifat alaqalim,* translated by Basil Anthony Collins. Reading, England: Centre for Muslim Contribution to Civilization, 1994.
8. Luqman Nagy. *The Book of Ibns*: The amazing sons of Islam. (Darus Salam publishers) Riyadh, Saudi Arabia, 2007
9. Ibn Fadlan, Ibn Fadlan and The Land of Darkness: Arab Travellers in the Far North, (Penguin Classics), 2012, p31
10. Ibn Fadlan, Ibn Fadlan and The Land of Darkness: Arab Travellers in the Far North, (Penguin Classics), 2012, p115
11. Ibid, p 62-71
12. Source: al-Bakrī, The Book of Highways and Kingdoms (Kitāb al-masālik wa-l-mamālik), Teaching Medieval Slavery and Captivity, retrieved from https://medievalslavery.org/africa/source-al-bakri-the-book-of-highways-and-kingdoms-kitab-al-masalik-wa-l-mamalik/
13. Muslim Heritage, Discover the Golden Age of Muslim Civilization, (Muslim Heritage), 2020, retrieved from https://muslimheritage.com/people/scholars/al-ijlia/
14. Salim Al-Hassani, Traveller and Explorers from a Golden Age, (Muslim Heritage), 2020, retrieved from https://muslimheritage.com/travellers-and-explorers/
15. Ibn Fadlan, Ibn Fadlan and The Land of Darkness: Arab Travellers in the Far North, (Penguin Classics), 2012, p 187-188.
16. Ibn Sa'id al-Maghribi – Muslim Heritage, Discover the Golden Age of Muslim Civilization, (Muslim Heritage), 2020, retrieved from https://muslimheritage.com/people/scholars/ibn-said-al-maghribi/
17. Tim Mackintosh-Smith, The Travels of Ibn Battuta, (Pic-

ador), 2002.

18. Rifa'a Rafi al-Tahtawi, An Imam in Paris: Account of a Stay in France by an Egyptian Cleric, (Saqi), 2011, p 263.
19. Juber Ahmed, "Eleven Muslim Travellers of the Past." (Muslims go travel), 2019, retrieved from https://muslimsgotravel.com/muslim-travellers-of-the-past/
20. Daniel Majchrowicz, Travelling to Acquire Knowledge, (Marginalia), 2014, retrieved from https://themarginaliareview.com/travelling-acquire-knowledge/

## Part 2: Basic Principles of Travel

1. Documented in *Sharh Zād al-Mustaqni'* by Mohammad al-Mukhtār ash-Sahanqīti.
2. Musnad Ahmad, hadith number 5/428,429.
3. Abu Hamid al-Ghazali, Ihya' 'Ulum al-Din: The Revival of the Religious Sciences. Islamic Book Trust 2015

## Part 3: Staying Connected During Travel

4. As-Sayyid Sabiq, Fiqh us-Sunnah, (International Islamic Publishing House), 1991, p44-46.
5. Fatwaa #061 – Substances which one can make Tayammum. (Darul Ifta New Zealand), 2021, retrieved from https://darulifta.org.nz/substances-which-one-can-make-tayammum/.
6. Mufti Muhammad Taqi Usmani, Contemporary Fatawa, (Maktaba Ma'ariful Quran), 2023, p144.

## Part 4: Staying Healthy While Travelling

1. Madiha Saeed, The Qur'anic Prescription: Unlocking the Secrets to Optimal Health, (Kube Publishing), 2022.
2. Mark Hyman, Food: What the Heck Should I Eat, (Little, Brown and Company), 2018.
3. Mark Hyman, How to Prevent a Food Emergency (Dr. Hyman), 2016, retrieved from https://drhyman.com/blog/2016/03/22/how-to-prevent-a-food-emergency-

and-a-giveaway/

4. Healthy Eating While Travelling (Tufts Health and Nutrition Letter), 2022, retrieved from https://www.nutritionletter.tufts.edu/healthy-eating/healthy-eating-while-travelling/
5. Frank Lipman, The New Rules of Aging Well, (Artisan), 2020.
6. Steven Pratt and Kathy Matthews, Superfoods: Fourteen Foods That Will Change Your Life, (Harper), 2004.
7. Mike Wiking, The Little Book of Lykke: Secrets of the world's happiest people (The Happiness Institute Series), (William Morrow), 2017.
8. Michael Pollan, The Omnivore's Dilemma: A Natural History of Four Meals, (Penguin), 2007.
9. Frank Lipman, 8 Ways to Fight Jet Lag and Enjoy Your Travels (Dr Frank Lipman, MD), 2022, retrieved from https://drfranklipman.com/2022/06/27/8-ways-to-fight-jet-lag-and-enjoy-your-travels/
10. Wittmann M, Dinich J, Merrow M, Roenneberg T. Social jetlag: misalignment of biological and social time. Chronobiol Int. 2006;23(1-2):497-509. doi: 10.1080/07420520500545979. PMID: 16687322.

## Part 10: Solo Travel as a Muslim

1. Gibson, J, Commuting to work in the US: facts and statistics, (Bankrate), 2024, retrieved from https://www.bankrate.com/insurance/car/commuting-facts-statistics/

## Further Reading

*Al-Kawthari, M. 2020. A Trip to the Land of Scholars and Saint In* the Company of Shaykh al-Islam Mufti Muhammad Taqi Usmani.

Burdick, Alan, Why time flies: a mostly scientific investigation.

Bron, M. 2019. Travel the World Without Worries: An Inspirational Guide to Budget and Adventure Travel (3rd Edition).

Campbell, J. 2015. The Bookshop Book. Little, Brown Book Group.

Drori, J. 2018. Around the World in 80 Trees. Laurence King Publishing.

Editors of Storey Publishing. 2018. Backpack Explorer: On the Nature Trail: What Will You Find? Storey Publishing.

Fries, H. 2018. Forest Bathing Retreat: Find Wholeness in the Company of Trees. Storey Publishing.

Fadlan, I., Lunde, P. 2012. Ibn Fadlan and the Land of Darkness: Arab Travellers in the Far North. Penguin Classics.

Hadjicostis, N. 2016. Destination Earth: A New Philosophy of Travel by a World Traveller. Bamboo Leaf Press.

Hussain, T. 2021. Minarets in the Mountains: A Journey into Muslim Europe. Brandt Travel Guides.
Jennings, K. 2012. Maphead: Charting the Wide, Weird World of Geography. Scribner; Illustrated Edition.

Khan, I. 1990. Indus Journey: A Personalized View of Pakistan. Chatto & Windus.

Kroll, D. 2021. Pacific Coasting: A Guide to the Ultimate Road Trip, from Southern California to the Pacific Northwest. Artisan, Illustrated Edition.

Knighton, C. 2021. Leave Only Footprints: My Acadia-to-Zion Journey Through Every National Park. Crown.

Lieber, R. 2009. Forest Meditations. Muir Woods Meditations.

Lonely Planet. 2020. The Family Travel Handbook. Lonely Planet.

Lockman, MC. 2016. Warning! Family Vacations May Be Hazardous To Your Health. Mary Clare Lockman.

Lamps, JM. 2020. Work, Save, Travel, Repeat: The Complete Guide to Amazing Budget Travelling. Independently Published.

Mohammad, F. 2016. The Productive Muslim: Where Faith Meets Productivity. Claritas Books.

McHenry, RS. Trip Tales: From Family Camping to Life as a Ranger. Huntley Avenue PressRechtschaffen, Stephan: Time Shifting: creating more time to enjoy your life.

Saeed, MM. 2022. The Qur'anic Prescription: Unlocking the Secrets to Optimal Health. Kube Publishing.

Soojung-Kim Pan, Alex, Rest: Why you get more done when you work less.

Smith, Irene and Van Der Hulst, Astrid, A book that loves you.

Usmani, MT. 1989. A Few Dyas in Al-Andalus Muslim Spain. White Fountain Publishing.

Wohlleben, P. 2019. The Secret Life of Nature: Trees, Animals and the Extraordinary Balance of All Living Things – Stories from Science and Observation (The Mysteries of Nature/ David Suzuki Institute, 3). Greystone Books.

# Index

## B



## C



## D

## E



## F



## G



## H



## I

## U



## V



## W



## Y



## Z